Copyright 2011 by:
Bob Stegall Publishing
P.O. BOX 83
Tuscumbia, AL 35674

ISBN 978-0-9834424-0-0

All rights reserved. The contents of this book, as a whole or in part, may not be reproduced without the expressed written consent of the author.

All references to names of Corporations, businesses, products, logos, brands, etc., are the property of their respective Trademark holders. We make no claim that they endorse or support, or underwrite this book "The Storyteller from Sugar Creek" in any way.

All Scripture references used are from the NIV Large Print Study Bible, 10th Annniversary Edition, copyright 1995 by the Zondervan Corporation; The Holy Bible, New International Version Copyright 1973, 1978, 1984 by the International Bible Society

The Story Teller

from Sugar Creek

by

Bob Stegall
"The Reverend Doctor Robert H. "Bob" Stegall"

These stories are written with appreciation for my soul mate, team player, and best friend: Kay Frances Ward Stegall.

And our children: Robert Patterson "Pat" Stegall
Maryjane Hean
Jennifer Diane Sun

THE STORY TELLER FROM SUGAR CREEK

FOREWORD

CHAPTER 1   BORN NEAR SUGAR CREEK
             A BABY BOY
             GRANDS WILL AND LORA STEGALL
             ROUTE HIGHWAY 45
             SUGAR CREEK FARM
             GRANDS BOB AND LILLIE PATTERSON
             TYING THE KNOT
             HUMBLE AND GOOD MANAGERS
             THE CRAWLING STEGALL BOYS
             LOVE, VICK'S SALVE AND SULFA DRUGS
             DOG TOWN
             GRANNY'S GARDEN

CHAPTER 2   STREAKING ON SUGAR CREEK
             KIN TO ADAM AND EVE
             MAN'S BEST FRIEND
             SHE TENDS HER FLOCK
             FATHERLY INFLUENCE
             ON MUDDY POND
             AS BUSY AS A BEE
             HAPPY AS A LARK

CHAPTER 3   THEM OLD DAYS
             THE MOCKINGBIRD
             CAN WE MEASURE SUFFERING?
             HEY, YOU ARE COOL
             THE HEART OF THE HAM
             THE TOWN CHARACTER
             LIKE A THREE RING CIRCUS
             THE CROSSIN'
             "PO' TOM"
             SEASONS OF THE HOLLY BUSH

CHAPTER 4   LIFE WISH LIST
             APRIL 15- IRS, IRA AND SRA
             AMERICA PAST THE CROSSROADS

DETOURS ON THE CHRISTMAS JOURNEY
ROME - PAST THE CROSSROADS
THANK GOD AND McDONALD'S
THE COOING OF A TURTLE DOVE
GAIN THE BEST FROM THE TEST
LOVE IS..........BEING THERE
WHO IS BOO RADLEY?

CHAPTER 5   FROM JUNE BUGS TO TRANSFORMERS
A FEAST OF MEMORIES
INSTANT, HOME GROWN OR BOTH?
THE PERFECT GIFT
AARON'S CHARIOT
A CONCRETE ODE TO JOHN
A CREAMY TRIBUTE TO WOODY
DEAR FRIEND
HELLO BROTHER, COVERING ARREARS
HAIL JOSEPH, FULL OF COMMITMENT

CHAPTER 6   YOU GOT THE BAMA BUZZARD
GOOD NEWS AT THE MARKET PLACE
WHAT NOT TO DO...
CROW'S ELBOW
HONK IF YOU LOVE JESUS
IN SENIOR YEARS
IN OUR PERSONAL SUFFERING
IN A WORLD OF TEMPTATIONS
IS A SQUIRREL OUT THERE YET?
A TALE OF LEAF BURNING
A BETTER PERSPECTIVE
A MIXED BAG

CHAPTER 7   PUT THE PLOW IN THE GROUND
A FATHER RESPONDS
CULTIVATING A THANKFUL SPIRIT
WHAT EVERY FATHER SHOULD KNOW
THE HOMECOMING
THE HOPE OF CHRISTMAS
A TEAR AND A SMILE
A SALUTE TO WILLIE FRANK
FAREWELL AND HELLO

FAMILIES RECOVERING
GOOD GRIEF

CHAPTER 8   BOTTOM LINE LIVING
HOMECOMING IS LIKE........
HAPPY THANKSGIVING
TEN GUIDES FOR CHURCH GROWTH
A TWO BUS CHURCH
A NEW BEGINNING
REMOTE CABIN FEVER
FAITH VERSUS FRUSTRATION
HEY COACH, GOT A MINUTE?
GETTING ON FIRST BASE
OLD ROADS AND NEW FRIENDS
"CAN I TAKE MY GUN TO CHURCH?"
UNSEARCHABLE RICHES OF CHRIST
A GOOD PATTERN FOR LIVING
THE QUEST FOR CHARACTER
THE GOOD OLE SUMMER TIME
THE GOLDEN GROWTH RULE
WHAT'S NEW?
LIGHT AND SHADOW
THIS IS THE PLACE!

CHAPTER 9   WHAT'S IN A NAME?
ANDY WAS A DANDY
THE GIFT OF WORK
GIVING A FATHER'S BLESSING
SEVEN PORTRAITS
A WINNING STRATEGY
PAPA'S GOLD WATCH
VOICES FROM THE PAST
PREPARING FOR HUMMINGBIRDS
THE CROSS AND THE CROWN
A TRAIL OF ROSE PETALS
AN EXAMPLE IS WHERE YOU FIND IT
THE WALKING BIBLE
HERE COMES MISS HETTIE
BLIND SPOTS
"HELLO? ANYBODY HOME?"

THE WAVE
MONDAY NIGHT AT BUSCH STADIUM
GOD BLESS THE CHILDREN

CHAPTER 10　WHO WILL SAY THE BLESSING?
PASTORAL LEADERSHIP IS……..
WHO ARE THE STEGALLS?
MY BEST FRIEND
HAVE SOME TURKEY AND GRAVY
"THE TEACHER"
THREE C'S OF SUCCESS
WHAT WOULD JESUS DRIVE?
KINKS IN THE HOSE
"WISH WE WERE THERE"
LITTLE FOXES THAT SPOIL THE VINEYARD
ROAD SPILL

CHAPTER 11　TO BE A MILLIONARE
I'LL THINK ABOUT THAT
TWO WHITE RIBBONS
WE GOT MAIL
THE HORROR COPE
THE LITTLE HOUSE
DEPOSITING AFFIRMATIONS
AS THE CROW FLIES
A FAIRY RING
THERE'S A SNAKE!
 MAY I BE EXCUSED?
A NEW COWBOY COMES TO TOWN
"HERE, BOB, HERE!"

Foreword

When someone asks me where I went to school, I reply, "The first college I attended was COF, College of Farming." I grew up on the banks of Sugar Creek that flowed through the farm south of Humboldt, Tennessee, in Gibson County. I was born on the farm in the little unpainted house, and learned there were four seasons in the year, with jobs to do in every season to be ready for the next season. In eighteen years one learns a lot from working with father, mother, brother, grandparents, cousins, aunts, uncles, neighbors, share croppers, hired hands, merchants, friends, bankers, etc.

The first church I served after graduating from Johnson Bible College was in Bells, Tennessee, just thirteen miles from the family and farm. It was also just thirteen miles from mother's deep freezer, canned fruits and vegetables, daddy's smoke house with cured pork, and Sugar Creek. The church asked me to do three services each week. There were two Sunday services, morning and evening, and a Wednesday night service. That required a lot of thinking, bible study, and praying. I looked for illustrations wherever I could find them.

I did not know about the Lectionary. Computers were not widely used in 1957, but there was television with history, funny stories and characters, and books. Some of my first illustrations were about Albert Schweitzer and his mission work. A major breakthrough for me was reading one of Clovis Chappel's books. He was a Methodist minister, raised on a farm in Tennessee. He told stories of his life and experience on the farm to illustrate his biblical stories in the pulpit. I still have three of his books in my library: <u>Sermons from Job</u>, <u>Sermons on the Lord's Prayer</u>, and <u>The Seven Last Words</u>.

    Kay, my soul mate, has always reminded me that sermons need good windows through which the congregation can see God's truth, the light of Christ, and reflections with the Holy Spirit. Jesus was a story teller. His messages were always in simple language, using everyday spoken words such as salt, leaven, seed, weeds, sheep, sowing, harvesting, two sons and a loving father, etc. God has given me many stories over the more than fifty years of preaching, teaching, and pastoral work. For years people have said, "Bob, you need to write a book of your stories." I have been writing them. Sugar Creek is the book. I hope you enjoy reading them as much as I have enjoyed telling them. Thanks to our daughter, Maryjane Hean for typing and editing my book of stories.

    In over fifty years of pastoral ministry, I have been taught and mentored by wise, skilled, and practical teachers. It is with gratitude that I write this book in appreciation for my professors of preaching: Dr. Fred B. Craddock, Johnson Bible College; Dr. Ronald Sleeth, Vanderbilt Divinity School; and Dr. Richard White, Lexington Theological Seminary. They have helped me fulfill the commission Dr. Jean Woolfolk gave our graduation class at Lexington Theological Seminary in 1978, "Preachers, put the fodder where the calves can get it."

Chapter 1
Born Near Sugar Creek

Sugar Creek

Clark was digging the red potatoes on that July morning, potatoes he had planted with Papa in late April on the banks of Sugar Creek, Gibson County, in West Tennessee. He kept looking toward the house and listening for the dinner bell. It was not noon, but Louise was in labor with their second child and he was ready to run and be by her side.

A neighbor from across the road, highway 45, was sitting with Louise during her labor. A man could only do so much, maybe boil some water when it was ordered. So he headed for the potato patch, within hollering distance of the house. Word had been sent to Dr. Penn in Humboldt, and he was on his way to help deliver and tie off the strings on the newborn.

Clark had already made a trip with the mules and wagon to Beare Ice and Coal Company at the railroad crossing in Humboldt to get some ice to comfort Louise. He bought a batch of lemons, too. In the July heat, the ice would cool her forehead, and the lemonade would quench her thirst. It was as close to snow cream as he could get in July. She loved snow cream.

It was hard to stay on your knees and pile the dug potatoes with so much on your mind. Sometimes he was digging potatoes and sometimes he was praying. You could do either on your knees in the fresh turned dirt. He was doing both. The potatoes were turned up in the sun for their first streaks of sunlight. Blue and Joe, the mules, were eating grass at the end of the rows, still hitched to the turning plow that lifted a harvest to feed a family for months to come.

"Clark, come to the house," was the call from the hill toward Sugar Creek. Clark jumped to his feet and ran toward his caller. He got there about the time Dr. Penn was wiping the blood off a brand new little boy. He said Louise had made it fine. She had a lot of pain but was doing fine.

Clark kissed Louise on the forehead and patted her hand. She looked at him and said, "It's a boy." She wanted a girl because her firstborn, Billy, was a boy. She wanted to sew and make dresses for a girl. She really wanted a boy and girl. Clark said, "I just thank God you are okay and the baby appears to be healthy." She looked him in the eyes and said, "Yes. Me, too. And he can wear dresses while he is little."

Naming a Baby Boy

They discussed the names they had planned, leaving out the girl's and sifting through the boy's. Finally, one came to the top like cream in a churn. Let's name him Robert Harold Stegall and call him "Bobby" for short. Stegall for the Stegalls. Robert for the Pattersons. Harold because it just sounds good, and maybe is a hint of a gift from God. They agreed it was good to have two boys, Billy and Bobby, July 10, 1934.

The baby grew and the dresses came in handy. It made it easier to change diapers, and there were plenty to change. His legs were not ideal for dresses but Mama wanted to show off both dresses and the new baby. From the waist to the knees they were

Patterson legs, a little chubby. The knees to the ankles were Stegall, thin, hairy, and strong. The glitch was the bowed legs.

There were numerous theories about the bowed legs. Maybe Mama's diet had been a little off in those lean years on the farm. Maybe Bobby was too fat and tried to walk too soon. Maybe God knew he was going to have a pony one day and he was born to ride. Maybe it was the weight from carrying too many of the rabbit dog Queen's puppies. Maybe it was a sign of some Indian heritage that he would make bows and arrows to hunt and fish. Maybe they were just made for walking, behind mules in the field, in plowed fields with scattered arrowheads, in towns and cities, colleges and schools, rest stops and bushes, sidewalks and church aisles, Israel and Greece, or to the outhouse. It would be a shame to cover those legs too long, and the dress made an admirable display of the walker practicing for decades of work and adventure.

The dress did serve on occasion as a security aid. For a while there was no water or well at the two-room house Daddy built on the acre and one half Papa and Granny sold them for one dollar. The first cooler was a hole he dug in the pasture with a posthole digger. It helped keep milk a few hours longer. Water was drawn from the well at Granny and Papa's house and carried in buckets back to the little house. What is a Mama to do with a crawling baby and a two year old when necessity sends her next door to fetch water with two buckets? The two year old had already put her pretty red shoes in the hot stove oven and roasted them. The baby was already pulling up and pulling things down. The dress became a perfect anchor for security purposes. Lift the bedstead and lower it on the corner of the dress. She watched the two year old on her errand. She listened for the anchored crawler's cry. She reasoned, "A little crying is better than a lotta hurtin'." Hardship always smiled when he passed Mama. She won his respect a long time ago.

A few pictures were made of the little boys by relatives and friends and given to Clark and Louise. One is in front of a car. They are standing behind the thin chrome bumper in front of the radiator grill. Both boys have their hands on the bumper of a new era. One boy has on short pants and the other wears a pretty white dress. Bobby is beginning to smile, talk, and point. Dresses are in their last days for him. Any day now he will be in revolt. He will say, "I want to wear britches like my brother." He always admired his brother. One wonders why pictures are seldom made of new parents. Love between a man and woman is a gift of God. Who would think they could raise children without hard work, help from God and family?

My Paternal Grandparents: Will and Lora Stegall

Will and Lora Stegall raised six children, five girls and a boy. Clarabell was the oldest. Next were the twins, Nina and Bess. Clark was sandwiched between Vera and Sue. When Will and Lora married, they moved to a big house near Mullins Road on Highway 45. Lora was a Mullins. She had two brothers. Joe lived in Dyersburg, Tennessee. Luther owned a grocery store on Mitchell Street in Humboldt.

It took a family to raise a family. Clarabell helped in the kitchen, making biscuits and cornbread. She watched the kids when Granny was in the garden picking peas and beans. Nina and Bess carried water from the creek to wash clothes. Vera and Clark went to the woods behind the house to get firewood for the stove and washpot. Sue, being the baby, just helped them all. Will was a truck farmer. He was busy with tomatoes and cabbage, cotton and corn, and taking care of the mules that pulled the wagons and plows.

The kids all went to Sanders Bluff School. It was a one-room school, about a mile from their house. When they asked to be excused they went to the woods. Only the parents would question the teacher's behavior. The guideline at home was if you get a whippin' at school, you will get one when you get home. No one wanted a double whopper in those days, and hold the fries for creamed potatoes at supper.

Route Highway 45

Will had some family that lived at Sanders Bluff and farmed. They were sharecroppers on the Sanders farm, Uncle Horace Stegall and his family. No one ever explained the connection but he had a bunch of boys. They were happy boys, played the guitar, French harp, and banjo. Sometimes you might see one of them at Birdsong's Grocery across the field from Sanders Bluff on Highway 45. Sometimes you could hear them on somebody's porch, just a pickin' and singin', smilin' and laughin'. World War II came. Uncle Horace's' family was never the same again. Thank God for music. It is a bridge over the good and bad.
The big house had carbide lights. It was a step

up from kerosene lamps. TVA and electricity had not made its way across the Tennessee Valley, but Highway 45 did. The old dirt road to Jackson gave way to a concrete highway, adaptable for cars, trucks and tractors. Will joined other farmers with his team of mules and dirt scoop to make a little extra money and help a good thing happen. Clark was a water boy. Tips were rare but tongues were abundant. He heard a lot of mule talk, but in a lifetime his children never heard him take the Lord's name in vain. Some things are better left in the barn.

   Aunt Tek was the only other Stegall who ever showed up. She came from Texas for a visit. Will's sister, no doubt. There was not much extra money for travel or postage. She was a nice lady, friendly and had a pleasant smile. Riding a train from Texas to Tennessee to see kinfolk is to be commended.

   When Highway 45 opened Will got interested in a farm closer to town. Sugar Creek ran through the block of land and it would be ideal for truck farming with some bottom land and sandy soil. There had been a rumor Humboldt might some day build a golf course on Highway 45 across from Mullins Road. Will never had much time for playing, and was ready to make a move up. He and Lora decided to buy the Sugar Creek farm and take on some more work projects. Having a closer ride to town carried a lot of weight in their decision since they planned to sell milk and butter, turnip greens and sweet potatoes.

Move to Sugar Creek Farm

It was a good move to Sugar Creek. The big house that came with the land was on the old dirt road to Jackson. They moved it up beside Highway 45. They moved it like a snail crawls. You need a mule, pulley, posthole digger, heavy posts, and lots of rope. Dig a hole a hundred feet away. Plant the post. Attach another post to the post. Tie the rope onto the house. Run it through the pulley and attach it to the standing post. Hitch the mule to the attached horizontal post and have the mule walk in a circle. Slowly it moves the house. There is no hope of "streaking" when you move a house at Sugar Creek. Your best bet is to try to think like a snail crawls. Slowly, no, slower. From the pyramids and Roman amphitheatres to moving houses and growing crops, how marvelous what human beings can accomplish with small tools and great purpose.

The front and side porch faced the highway. You could sit in the swing and watch the world go by. More and more models of cars and trucks coming from Three-Way or headed for Jackson. Wagon loads of cabbage and tomatoes headed for the trucks and box cars by the fruit sheds at the railroad crossing. Wagons loaded with cotton pulled by mules trotting to a unique rhythm created by the eight shoed hooves dancing up the road from the field to Mr. Kizer's cotton gin, with the sound of money in the air. And the bonus from Mr. Kizer's hand, a free pencil that said "Kizer Cotton Gin", and a tablet for writing figures. Sometimes a kerosene lantern hung on the back of a wagon, heralding a long day's work, going home, trotting into the dusk, sitting on the check from the cotton gin, thinking about supper time and loving faces around a table. By the grace of God hard times can be good times, too.

Lora and Will got busy making their house a home. With five children they planned every day to give them another reason to want to come home again, back to the nest. Lora planted a garden and canned vegetables in season. Will slopped hogs for cold weather killing time, and built a smoke house, a place to hang the sugar cured hams and shoulders. They built a hen house to gather eggs for breakfast or baking cakes. They planted fruit trees and the orchard had pears, apples and peaches. Sometimes apples were cut and dried on the tin roofed shed for making fried apple pies in the winter. Then there were the bee hives, with bees pollinating the trees and crops, storing up honey for a sweet treat on a buttered biscuit. Going home again was a blessing.

My Maternal Grandparents: Bob and Lillie Patterson

The Pattersons lived closer to town than the Stegalls, less than a mile up Highway 45 and a mile and a half if you took the old dirt road to Jackson. Bob and Lillie rented the land and farmed. The house was big enough for four children and became the gathering place for the Wrays, Pooles and Pattersons. The large families came by wagon, bringing food to cook and quilts and blankets for sleeping. The kids played hide and seek in the yard, climbed trees, rolled wagon hoops and pitched horseshoes. They practiced cooking by making mud pies and roasting ears of fresh corn over an open fire.

Sarah was the oldest. She liked to dress up, stay out of the sun. When she grew up, she moved to Memphis and became a model for Goldsmith's Department Store. Louise was a hard worker and worked in the fields beside her Daddy, suckering and tying tomato plants to stakes, cutting cabbage and chopping cotton. She wore a bonnet and long sleeves to keep her skin protected from the scorching sunshine. Robert McDonald was the only boy. He was handsome and gentle spirited. He helped out around the house, fed the mules and watered the cows, but never aspired to be a farmer. He liked to socialize, play music and dance. When he returned from the war, he worked in the City Café, Firestone Store, and taped music for merchants and friends. The whole town knew Robert. Edna was the youngest child. She helped around the house and enjoyed being the baby of the family. She had a knack for arranging pretty flowers and being friendly. One day she would own her own business, Alamo Flower Shop.

Bob grew crops in the bottom land alongside Little Sugar Creek. Daughter Louise worked in the fields, often beside a hired hand, a funny and friendly man, Odell Todd. Clark saw Louise across the creek and thought she was pretty. He liked to plow crops along the creek banks because he could see Louise.

Neighbors helped each other, filling in the gaps and hard places. The Stegall's cow went dry. No milk, butter, or buttermilk. Clark's mother sent him to the Patterson's to get milk. Their cow was in season and there was milk to spare. Clark liked the trip. He could ride his pony and see Louise all at the same time. He loved to do both. Louise thought Clark was nice and handsome. She returned his friendliness with a smile. One thing led to another, and one day they married and made their home between Big Sugar Creek and Little Sugar Creek.

Tying the Knot

They eloped to be married in Corinth, Mississippi. Clark sneaked some of Granny's Plymouth Rock hens from the barn lot and sold them to buy gas, pay the courthouse and judge. Aunt Bess and Uncle Earl Hegler went along as witnesses. His sister could stand up for him when he broke the news to Granny and Papa. Louise had to stand up for herself. But Clark stood with her. There were a match that time proved a blessing of God. They had just enough change to eat cheese and crackers on their wedding day. It became a family tradition every November 22. God is good.

The newlyweds rented an apartment in town. They lived in a house near Wray's Grocery in North Humboldt, between the Trenton Highway and North 17th Street. Clark got a job as a night watchman for the fruit sheds at the crossing. He carried a small pistol.

Their first child, William Clark Stegall, Jr. was born September 15, 1932. He carried the Stegall name to the third generation. Will, William Clark, and now, Junior. He was a good boy. They called him Billy.

Clark could not turn loose of the farm. He walked from town to the farm, out South 17th Street, across Rosehill Cemetery, across Little Sugar Creek. Papa and Granny sold Clark and Louise 40 acres of land on the south side of Big Sugar Creek. They deeded them one and a half acres beside their home for them to build their house.

   Clark and Louise moved in with Papa and Granny, planted a crop and started construction on their house. It was a simple house, three rooms and a long kitchen added on to the back. It had low rafters. The boarding was vertical, wide 10-inch boards and a 4-inch board sealing the joints. The roof was covered with rolled roofing. The front porch was held up with jointed two-by-fours. With a lot of love, they made a house a home.

   Clark and Louise loved to grow things. Clark planted corn and cotton, cabbage and tomatoes in the fields. Louise planted day lilies and iris, gardenias and daisies in the yard.

   They groomed a nest where two boys, like two little birds, could grow and flap their wings. They added a chicken house for fresh eggs and fried chicken. They built a smokehouse for curing and storing meat from pigs raised on the farm. They had a garden, and harvested food from the fields. They bought sugar, flour, meal, coffee, tea and sometimes candy, with money from selling milk and butter, turnip greens and strawberries. One time they traded a country ham for a case of canned salmon. It was a feast for weeks. The two little birds never went hungry.

Humble and Good Managers

Dimes were scarce in those depression years. The philosophy was "don't throw out the back door more than you bring in the front door." A different version was "waste not and want not," or, "it is not how much you make but how much you spend that makes the difference." Then there is, "a penny saved is a penny earned."

Billy and Bobby were nurtured in a family spirit on the farm. You didn't have to wait until suppertime to talk to your Mama and Daddy. You would see them at breakfast, dinner and supper. Often you were in the fields with them, riding on a cotton sack, groundslide, wagon or mule. Family time was not by appointment. It was all the time. Nurture was consistent.

The boys' first pair of store bought leather shoes were bronzed when they grew out of them. They were displayed over the years on a table along with pictures of the growing family tree. Clark and Louise picked turnip greens in the winter, pulling the snow back with their hands, to pick the greens for their three favorite stores in town: Bethsheares on Main Street, Mullins on Mitchell Street, and Wray Brothers on North 17th Street.

Maybe the shoes were bronzed to hide the yellow stains. Perhaps it was the cut open toe, that allowed a few more months of growth. It could have been they were firsts for one year olds. No doubt it was a celebration of some physical memory that Mama and Daddy had made with Billy and Bobby their first year. No doubt it was a bronzed blessing, a timeless thank offering for seeing two little boys grow healthy through their first year. And, it would be a good tool of humble beginnings to chase away pride when it became too rowdy. It is a reminder, a haughty spirit is not a good goal. It was still hard for the boys to not puff up a bit when they explained the shoes. "No, we are not twins, but these are our first shoes when we were one year old that Mama and Daddy cut turnip greens to buy." These treasured shoes are not for sale. They are priceless memories of loving parents and survival in depressions years.

The Crawling Stegall Boys

One can make up endless stories around those bronzed shoes. Here is one called, "Crawling on Sugar Creek." Well, you can see the soles of those shoes are not worn. The wear is on the toes. These shoes were not made for walking. They were made for crawling. The boys' Mama and Daddy took them to the field everyday. While the parents picked tomatoes or chopped cotton the kids crawled between the rows. They raced each other and scratched-off in the middles. They sputtered and spat, their little engines a-roaring. Word spread among the neighbors and crowds gathered in the field alongside Sugar Creek. One day there was a tie in the crawl race, and they busted a watermelon to celebrate the feat. Neighbors pitched their pennies in a hat to have the "crawling shoes" bronzed to capture the moment forever. The shoes are a tribute to "the crawlin' Stegall boys."

The boys loved the barns. Clark built a barn, exactly like Papa's barn right beside it, with about twenty feet between them. Both faced Highway 45 from a hill. There was a pond below the hill, by the Catalpa tree. Clark built the barn there for watering his mules. Working mules drink a minimum of three times a day: morning, noon, and night.

As the boys advanced in walking and running skills they migrated to the barns. Feed the mules hay and corn. Break off the brown grains of corn damaged by worms, so the mules won't get sick. The pigs ate the bad corn, but pigs feast where other animals foul. Throw hay in the stable for the mules and put corn in their trough. Leave the cow in the pasture at night. Don't throw all the corn cobs away. They may come in handy. Shut the gates. Pull off your shoes at the door.

Love, Vick's Salve, and Sulfa Drugs

Dr. Harold Barker diagnosed me with double pneumonia when I was in the first grade. Both lungs were infected and had fluid. He prescribed a sulfa drug and told Mother and Daddy we could thank the Germans for that blessing. It was a timely statement because we were in World War II with the Germans. I was six years old, so it was the winter of 1940 or 1941. I know it was winter because I got a Daisy BB gun for Christmas.

Mother rubbed my chest in Vick's Salve. Daddy put a tea kettle on a hot plate beside my bed. The steam was supposed to moisturize the room and help me breathe. I lost my appetite for a while. One day Daddy asked, "Son, is there anything you think you can eat?" I said, "Daddy, I want a hamburger with mustard." He went to town and brought back hamburger meat, buns and mustard. I ate a whole hamburger, but the mustard tasted funny. I loved mustard on biscuits, buns or whatever. But the mustard left a taste in my mouth that wasn't good. Maybe it was a conflict with the sulfa drug or the smell was hard on my nose or lungs. Anyway, I didn't really enjoy mustard for two or three years. It is still my favorite garnish on sandwiches.

It was boring being sick and staying in bed, but I was blessed. My teacher, Miss Nichols, and my first grade class sent me some gifts for Christmas. Two or three weeks before Christmas, Bess, our neighbor, would come and sit by my bed and talk. She brought a package wrapped in white paper about the size of a short hot dog. She would shake it and say, "I bet you can't guess what this is." It rattled like dried peas in a pod, but I didn't have a clue that it was a round box of BB's.

There was a damson tree outside my bedroom window, and a mockingbird did a lot of singing from the branches. I wanted to shoot my BB gun so bad. Finally, I got bold enough to shoot BB's out the window and through the screen. The mockingbird was a tempting target but I was a bad marksman. I really learned an early lesson about grace from experience. I never hit the mockingbird, and Mother and Daddy never whipped me for shooting holes in the screen. Screen could be replaced on windows for very little money. I was a pretty big financial investment because of my bout with pneumonia, and it was a joy to see my mischief again. To this day I never recall a day when there was not a mockingbird singing in the yard. Sometimes it is a blessing of God's grace to miss your target.

For several weeks I looked out of the bedroom window. The weather was freezing in January. Billy and my cousins found some winter ways to pass time. They skated on a sheet of ice in front of the smokehouse. The ground was low and grass was gone. Water stood and waited to be changed to ice. My big brother, Bill, and cousins William Harvey, George, and Buck ran to the ice and slid on the wintry carpet. I enjoyed watching them compete in country olympics. They brought me stories of skating on the frozen pond and pools in Sugar Creek. Seeing them have fun and hearing their stories gave me another reason to want to get well. It worked for later I could say, " Been there. Done that."

Dog Town

One of the scary things I remember from my window was about the Mad Dog. Everybody in the neighborhood had a dog. Mr. Owens called it Dogtown. We had bird dogs, rabbit dogs, coon dogs, watch dogs, pet dogs, and stray dogs. The dreaded horror was of a mad dog. One night the dogs barked. Neighbors went out on their porches to evaluate the situation. Joe Erwin called from his front porch, "It's a mad dog." Rabies was deadly to man and beast. Joe Erwin fired his 12-gauge shotgun and yelled, "Clark, he's comin' your way." Daddy got his gun and knelt by my bed, looking out the window. Walter Waller joined the watch. Another shot was fired and they had a dead dog in the yard. His head was cut off and sent to Jackson for testing for rabies. It was a neighborhood victory that was celebrated with a Rook game and popcorn.

By March I was pretty well over the double pneumonia. Dr. Barker said it would be better to keep me out of school and start over in the first grade next year. I enjoyed the time to get acquainted with new neighbors, the Wallers and the McLemores. Both families moved from farms near Milan, Tennessee. Proctor and Gamble had bought up properties to develop the Milan Arsenal for making weapons to be used by the United States of America in World War II. Many people from the area would get jobs in the defense work. We got some wonderful neighbors when the Wallers and McLemores moved to our neighborhood to farm. Mr. And Mrs. James P. McLemore had a daughter, Gertrude, and a son, James, Junior. Maude and Amos Waller had five boys: Nat, Haywood, Newman, Walter, and Glen. Four boys served in the war and all returned home safely.

Newman loved wrestling and invited Billy and me to go to the Armory at Jackson, Tennessee to watch Monday night wrestling. The bad guy was "Rowdy Red Roberts". The good guy was Herb Welch. Herb always won at the last minute but Red Roberts was a bugger. He bent every rule in his favor and knew how to get the audience involved in shouting and yelling against his opponent. One night my favorite cowboy, Sunset Carson, was the referee. Rowdy Red was still just as mean. Later, I heard the three drove down from Nashville in the same car. There was a lesson in that...

Granny's Garden

Granny's garden was between the barn and the smokehouse. It was next to the pasture where the mules and cow grazed beside the road that went to Sugar Creek. She added a fence around her garden to keep any pigs or livestock from gathering her harvest. The chickens had permission to enter the garden as long as they didn't eat the seeds at planting time. Eggs and chickens were a big part of the family food supply, so anything they raised would eventually show up in the kitchen.

I doubt Granny ever bought a head of lettuce. It cost too much money, and she provided other leafy foods from the garden. Turnip greens were as regular as the sunrise. She specialized in pole beans, and the poles were canes that were cut from the banks of Sugar Creek. Sweet potatoes were a regular crop on the farm, as well as cabbage, tomatoes, Irish potatoes, and strawberries. The garden provided onions, carrots, radishes, cucumbers, peppers, black-eyed peas, crowder peas, and sweet corn. Very few people had permission to enter her garden, especially boys who always were looking for something to do. She kept an eye out the kitchen window on her grocery supply.

One fall she asked for our help in gathering the turnip crop. Turnips kept well under their purple and white covers, but they would shrivel up and dry if they were exposed over long periods of time. She had a plan for preserving the turnips for Christmas and through the cold winter months. "Boys, dig a big hole in the ground," she said. Then we gathered the turnips and piled them in the hole on a bed of straw. We added more straw and then piled the dirt on top. In winter you could go to the garden, rake back the snow, dig in the dirt and pull out turnips- cold, firm, colorful, and as tasty as a turnip can be. Sometimes she would sell a bushel of those precious turnips to buy flour, meal and sugar.

    Fertilizer came from the barn. It was processed by the mules, cows, and pigs. It was in abundant supply, and could be plowed into the ground in the fall to enrich the soil for the spring planting. The vegetables always tasted good, each with their own flavor. I doubt any original flavors were altered by the rich barnyard and stall contributions. Nothing ever went to waste on the farm. No one called animal droppings waste. It was a part of the food and supply chain. Ultimately everything went back into the soil, one way or another.

    Feeding a family was a daily challenge. What Granny did in the garden was something she had cultivated over the years. You can't cook what you don't have. Papa and Granny learned lessons and gained wisdom from their childhood and life experiences. People got married and had children, not because they had everything, but because they believed God blessed the hands and hearts of those who loved, worked, and managed well. Having three good meals a day means you have to find the way.

Chapter 2
Streaking on Sugar Creek

Streaking on Sugar Creek

Sugar Creek was the getaway place for the boys. Billy's friend, Ben, came out to see us one day, and we went to the creek. There was a sandy beach bank in the curve on the north side where water swirled in heavy rains and deposited sand a grain at a time. We played a while in the sand and decided to dig a pit for escape in case we were shelled or a bomb dropped from an airplane. We were thinking World War II because that news still surrounded us. There was a single hole at the top of the pit, and we were six feet down. Suddenly it began caving in on us, and we barely escaped. Sometimes boys do not think to measure consequences. Sometimes men do not recall when they thought like boys. Sand may build a grain at a time. Sand can fall by the yards.

Quicksand was soft sand well watered by the rain and drainage upstream. We raced to the creek after rains to wade in water, swim in fresh filled fishing holes, and walk in the quicksand. Quicksand was disguised. You walked and suddenly your feet went down in the sand and you felt you were being swallowed. It was as scary as watching "The Mummy Walks Again" at the Plaza theatre on Saturday afternoon. Sometimes you were so deep you could not lift your feet out of the sand. That's when you lie down, and pull yourself free by crawling toward the bank. You need a helping hand. I'll bet sometime and somewhere someone said, "Oh, I can do it myself." They left no tombstone and no one knows where they are buried today.

I got saved in Sugar Creek. After a good rain

the boys ran to the creek to swim. There were four of us: Billy, Buck (our cousin), Wink (our neighbor), and me. There was a good fishing and swimming hole in the curve above the bridge where the water spun when it ran fast and hit the bank. Wink brought a rubber inner tube that was used to inflate a tire on cars or trucks. It made a good swimming float. I was having a good time floating with the tube since I had not learned to swim. The other three guys could swim, and floating made me feel upgraded. I recall someone's arm hitting the tube in one of their strong strokes. The tube flipped and I went under the water. I came back up the third time, and our cousin, Buck, grabbed my arm and pulled me to the bank. I got saved and Buck was one of my favorite cousins. No, not cuss-sins. COUSINS! Aunt Bess and Uncle Earl's boy.

Kin to Adam and Eve

Streaking on Sugar Creek was an experience Aunt Buddy never let us forget. One day we went to the creek to celebrate a reunion with our cousins. It had not rained in days and the creek was dry. There were no water holes or quicksand. After jumping off the bridge into a sand pile a few times, boredom set in. Someone said, "Let's go down the creek all the way to North Forked Deer River." It was about three or four miles away, and we knew cool water would be running there. We reduced our travel gear to zero and left our clothes under the bridge. We began walking. The sand was so hot on that August day, we ran from shady patch to shady patch where willow tree shadows cooled the sand and our feet. We made the trip naked as Jaybirds. Aunt Buddy never let us forget our stupidity in the boast that we went "Streaking on Sugar Creek". We proved we were kin to Adam and Eve.

Man's Best Friend

A famous saying is "A dog is a man's best friend." Mr. Owens called our neighborhood on the farm "Dog Town." He was a World War I Veteran. They said, "He was gassed in the war." He sat by his window, read the paper, listened to the radio, and smoked Old Gold cigarettes he rolled with two fingers. Each evening he came to our house and brought the Commercial Appeal Newspaper for our family to read. He came at suppertime and filled us in on the days' activities. He talked about all the dogs in our neighborhood since they entertained him all day by doing dog things. I learned from Mr. Owens that famous claim of fellowship, "A dog is a man's best friend."

Queen was our family dog. She was a hound dog and had a big litter of puppies. Daddy made a picture of her offspring and had me to sit on the ground with her and try to hold the puppies still for the camera. The picture turned out good of me, and the puppies. And I teased Daddy later about how one of my first pictures was of me working as a handyman. I guess it took.

Scooter was my bird dog when I was in High School. We hunted quail in the winter. He and I missed the limit of six by one, on a hunt one day between Christmas and New Year's Day. Scooter was my buddy. When Kay and I started dating, Scooter had to make sure he was still my best friend. While Kay and I sat in the swing in the yard, Scooter came up and put his head between us and looked hard at both of us. Kay rubbed his head and talked with him.

That day Scooter became woman's best friend, too. In fact, all three of us became best friends.

Praise God for a wise teaching fulfilled that day as Proverbs 18:24 says, "One who has friends must show oneself friendly." Here puppy. Good dog! Point! Fetch!

She Tends Her Flock

Granny tended her cows as carefully as she did the giant wood burning stove in her kitchen. Both were links to a bountiful table, even in depression days. Bringing back a pail of milk from the barn was a prelude to her standing near the churn, patting butter in a wooden mold. At breakfast, freshly made butter anointed by the design of a blooming flower carved in the wooden mold invited a steaming mammoth biscuit to a joint adventure. No one would ever have imagined the cows at the barn and stove in the kitchen had anything in common, but Granny proved them wrong, over and over again.

The prophet Isaiah patted the mold of promise in poetry when he foretold the glory of the Lord to be revealed in the birth of a king. Isaiah connected the shepherd's tender loving care with laughter and fulfillment at God's table of plenty. A blooming flower on an ancient mold of sacred prophecy says, "He tends his flock like a shepherd; He gathers the lambs in his arms and carries them close to his heart; He gently leads those that have young." Isaiah 40:11

Granny was the mother of five girls and one boy. Her prayer was that she would live to see them all grown. She tended her cows in the morning and evening. She tended her children day in and day out until all were grown. She blended the pasture and the porch with skills that even words of poetry stumble to tell. Many a preacher tasted the freshly made butter from the cows, and smiled with her tended flock at Sunday dinner. McDonald's is great, but I would not swap all the McDonald's in the world for one meal like Granny's.

Prayer: Great Shepherd, help me to blend the work of my hands with joys of my heart. Bless those who share the hope of blooming flowers at tables where innocents feed.

Fatherly Influence

Mr. Waller had five boys. Nat was a farmer, the oldest. The military draft passed him by so that he could help feed and clothe people. In World War II, the Milan Arsenal took the Waller's farm for land on which to make the weapons of war. Haywood, Newman, Glenn, and Walter all served in the war and returned home. I saw a movie, 'The Sullivans', with all the brothers walking on the clouds of heaven, and I still thank God that the four Waller brothers all came back home to their Dad and Mom, Mr. Amos and Miss Maude.

The foxes got into Mr. Waller's hen house. He got his shotgun, stood on the back steps of his house, and shot both barrels through the hen house door. Next morning, he found three dead hens and no foxes. As we laughed at his story, we all learned not to shoot into the dark. They built a new house across from us and dug a tornado shelter in the dirt bank. He said, "Come on over when the wind blows hard." Miss Maude kept her flowers there in the winter.

The Wallers had the first T.V. in the neighborhood, black and white, the screen about the size of a plate. I strayed over to their house about 6 o'clock in the evenings. John Cameron Swayze reported the news. The puppets, Kukla, Fran, and Ollie came on next. Mr. Waller had a basket with Dentyne chewing gum on a table, and he always offered Billy and me a chew while we watched T.V.

Mr. Waller was a good man, good husband, good father, good neighbor, and good citizen. He was a good example in a lot of ways. It is not always the lecture or sermon we remember. Sometimes it's another down to earth, practical, and caring fatherly influence. When I drive through Rosehill Cemetery, I am in awe at the tombstones that mark my good fatherly influences—Mr. Waller, Daddy, Papa, Granddaddy, and many other good men. A good man is part of God's plan. A few good men can be good. A bunch of good men can be better.

On Muddy Pond

The muddy pond was down the hill from the barn on the road to Sugar Creek. The barn housed the farm animals, and stored the corn and hay for their food. We had two mules, Red and Joe, and a cow, and a bunch of hogs. The animals often ate bonus food in front of the stables and crib door, where they begged for more. Their standing there created a mess that found its way down the hill to the pond when it rained. We always had a muddy pond.

The pond was the water supply for our farm animals. After lunch we would take the mules to the pond for a drink before we went back to the field to plow. Sometimes the mules purposely delayed the return to work by walking out into the pond where they stood knee deep, slowly drinking their fill. There were times we had to wade out in the pond to get them by the bridle because they enjoyed the water cooling their legs on a hot July day.

The pond was my first fishin' hole. There was a Catalpa tree that grew on the bank. It grew big green leaves where butterflies laid their eggs so the hatch could feast on the huge heart shaped leaves. We called the hatch "tawby worms." They were two to three inches long, black with yellow stripes, and had a radar-like antenna on their tail. They were good catfish bait. You loaded it in the tail, through the body with the tip of the hook out of the head. The catfish went crazy over a "tawby worm." One day there was a school of baby catfish near the surface of the water. I dropped in worm, and the mama snapped it up quick. I let her go back to the babies. After all, tomorrow is another day.

My first rafting was on that Muddy Pond. In elementary school I was in a play written by Mark Twain. It was about Tom Sawyer, a story of a boy growing up in Missouri. I had a singing part in the play. I played one of the boys who was trying to get a turn at helping paint the fence. I presented a corncob pipe I had made and sang in a luring voice, "Here's a pipe made from a corncob." It is my only lifetime public singing solo. I went home and celebrated by building a raft made of Catalpa tree fence posts

Daddy had made. I stood on the raft and pushed out from the bank, pretending it was the Mississippi River, like the boy and runaway slave in the story.

I never cross the Mississippi River that I don't remember what I learned on Muddy Pond from animals, nature, school, friends, and plays about making transitions. Someone always wants to rush or push you in life. It is good to know when it is your turn.

Just As Busy As a Bee

When we dropped off the grandchildren at Montessori School while on vacation in El Paso, it brought back memories of when I attended Bee School on the farm. The bee hives were in the orchard next to the pasture. Bees appeared on clover, bitter weeds, apple trees, sometimes on me, and wherever they chose to go.

This spring we were planning our family vacation to Hawaii. I was on the phone with the children, back and forth, leaving messages-- "Call me when you get home", etc. Our daughter said, "Daddy has a bee in his bonnet." That put a frame of reference around my buzzy activity. They remembered Granny working in the field, wearing a homemade bonnet to protect her face and neck from the hot sun. A bee got in the bonnet and she went into a hand waving running fit. The word was "slow down Dad."

Catching lightning bugs was a good after dark competition. Get a jar with a lid. Run to the light. Open the lid and catch the bug when the light goes on. Don't let the caught bugs out with the new bug. After the game, check who has the most bugs and who has the brightest bug lantern. It was a good after dark game to let the supper of mustard greens, fried potatoes, country ham and corn bread settle before bedtime.

Catching a bee was different from catching a lightning bug. The bee was always busy. It was gathering nectar for the hive. The drone had passed through and flown to the moon. The queen was providing the next generation. The workers were busy making honey combs and honey for the winter months ahead. I learned not to interfere with the worker bee. The only time I ever got stung was when I got in the way. Actually, I became a "worker bee." I love the hive, mission, honey and other workers.

Paul encourages bee workers, "...be steadfast, immoveable, always abounding in the work of the Lord, knowing your labor is not in vain."
1 Corinthians 15:58. Come on bees. Let's be...

Happy As a Lark

One day, Daddy gave me my first dollar bill. With excitement I ran up the road to Odell and Margie's house to show them my good fortune. I pulled the dollar bill out of the bib of my overalls, and as we laughed, they teased me about my prosperity. Odell and Margie lived in an unpainted house. They were sharecroppers for the Waller family on a ten acre farm along the banks of Little Sugar Creek. They had a little dog named Fido that had everything it needed. The three were as happy as larks.

A few years later after I had graduated from college, I was taking a walk back home on the farm to feast on memories. Odell and Margie had moved to another unpainted house and were sharecroppers with the Byrd family. While walking toward the railroad I saw Odell plowing a mule pulling a one- row plow in a field between Big Sugar Creek and Little Sugar Creek. It was a thrill to see my childhood friend again. While we laughed and talked he pulled a one hundred dollar bill out of the bib of his overalls and said, "Look what I got, Bobby!" He was as happy as a lark.

… *Chapter 3*
Them Old Days

Them Old Days

    We did not fly the flag on the fourth of July because we did not have one. Daddy and Mother did pay taxes, and supported our neighbors who were veterans or had family in service. We did have rabbit traps to supplement the supper tables, and I grew up listening to stories of how Franklin D. Roosevelt started the Civil Conservation Corps to help lift us out of a 'Great Depression.'

    Mr. and Mrs. Parker brought a new 4th of July idea to our neighborhood. They made a pot of stew and invited all the neighbors for lunch. Sometimes it was chicken stew, and sometimes it was squirrel stew. One year we thought about barbecuing Jimmy, our little pet pig, but we could not overcome the emotional barrier. On the fourth of July, I stopped plowing with my favorite mule, Red, about 11 a.m. I rode Red to the barn, fed him a corn lunch, and went to the house to wash up for the neighborhood stew.

    The flag I remember most was in front of the elementary school in Humboldt. Kay and I both saluted that flag each morning in school with our classes. To this day I look for it as I go back home and drive down Main Street. In the middle of the street, at the corner of the school, was a huge statue. I rode around it on my bicycle to and from school. Later, I learned it was a statue of the 'Gray Ghost', General Nathan Bedford Forrest. He was later moved out of the street to Bailey Park. A few years ago, I learned that Forrest City, Arkansas, and Forrest Gump were named after him.

When I see the flag in the sanctuary during in worship, I always think of Bruce Smith. He served in the Navy, and shooed the pigeons out of the steeple here at the church. He was one of the kitchen buddies with Jimmy and Shorty. We dedicated the flag in honor of Bruce, and all who served for the freedom and democracy of our country.

Today we fly the flag at our house on special days of remembrance and observance. We will fly our flag on the forth of July weekend. There will be a span of lifetime memories flapping in the wind. One thing is for sure. We all stand on the shoulders of a brave and sacrificial multitude past, present, and even future. I pray every day, "May America bless God"- a prayer for what is given and what can be.

The Mockingbird

Roy Acuff sang, "Listen to the Mockingbird" on the Grand Ole Opry. I listened to the mockingbird when I had double pneumonia while in the first grade at Humboldt Elementary School. Dr. Harold Barker put me to bed and prescribed what they called "Sulfa Drug". It was at the beginning of World War II, and Dr. Barker said that we could thank the Germans for developing the drug. A lot of people died of pneumonia. It was called "The Old Man's Friend", silently taking him out of this world. Mine was double, in both lungs, and I am thankful I did not leave this world.

We lived in an unpainted house. Well, it was barely painted. It was wide planks, nailed vertical with strips covering the joints. The color was more of a whitewash. The bedroom was next to a Damson Plum tree, and the mockingbird came and sang to me from the Damson tree. We had electricity, and mother and daddy hooked up a hot plate by the side of my bed. They put Vick's Salve in a tea kettle, and turned the nozzle toward me. It steamed the room and was meant to soften the crud in my lungs and nose. No doubt, it worked.

    My appetite was low, and the only thing I imagined I could eat was a hamburger. Daddy went to town and bought some hamburger meat, buns, and mustard. I loved mustard, and could eat mustard and biscuits most any time. I will never forget the taste of the mustard. It was more than I could tolerate. It made me sick to my stomach, and seemed to mess up my breathing. I could taste the mustard in the bottom part of both lungs. I guess it was the afterglow of the Vick's Salve vapors. I am thankful my taste for mustard whole-heartedly returned.

    I still listen to the mockingbird. I sit in the swing on the porch most every evening-- listening, remembering, and learning. The mockingbird frequently goes to the highest limb on the Cedar tree. There is barely enough for it to grasp, so it sways without wind blowing. Someone said that a mocking bird sings as a territorial song, "This is my land, my stand, so don't intrude." Our mockingbird builds its nest every year in the Texas Honeysuckle. The thick vine is border control, and any intruder meets a fight in flight. The hummingbird is allowed to come and go for a brief taste from a blossom. Besides that, with a fast hummingbird, even a mockingbird knows when to hold them and when to fold them. I still listen.

Can We Measure Suffering?

Growing up on the farm in West Tennessee included hauling produce to the Farmer's Market 85 miles west to Memphis. When I was eleven years old, we began making two and three trips a week in the summer when our cabbage, tomatoes, cucumbers, and bell peppers were harvested. We arrived about 9 p.m. and tried to sell and deliver our vegetables by 8 a.m. to head home for another day. It was at night that I was introduced to big city life. There are many memories of people I saw and learned about over the years.

One memory is of a man who had no legs. He sat on a sled-like board with roller skate wheels under each corner. He had the luxury of a cushion to pad the surface. He propelled himself with his hands holding two blocks of wood. The blocks had pieces of old leather belts attached to help him hold on and give his hands some relief. He could skate across the asphalt parking lot as fast as other men could walk. His quiet endurance and steadfast attitude was a lesson about suffering to a boy who loved to play Tarzan and swing on grapevines at Sugar Creek.

At the Last Supper, Jesus said to his disciples, "This do in remembrance of me." A few hours later a Godly man would be accused of causing chaos. He would be ridiculed, stripped of his clothes, forced to carry a cross in the streets, and nailed to a cross between two men being punished for their crimes against society. He suffered and died, and God fulfilled the words of Jesus' cousin, "Behold, the lamb of God who takes away the sins of the world." At the Lord's Table, we remember we are bought with a price, and the wood beneath his hands propels us on our faith journeys. There is no leather sleeve; so, hold tight.

Hey, You Are Cool

People have always been creative at keeping cool. Adding screens to windows that could be opened preceded electricity. Even those who lived in log cabins built breeze ways between rooms. Some called them dog trots, but really they were breeze ways. The dogs just liked the breezes.

Uncle Carl was a mechanic. He kept us cool. He built a box fan with boards on four sides, a fan from an old car in the middle, and an electric motor to draw air into the house. It was noisy, but it was a blessing on hot summer days and nights. Sometimes we watered down a cloth potato sack and hung it across the square box for the fan to pull air into the house. We took turns watering down the sack cloth.

As time progressed, we voted on adding an air conditioner to the sanctuary at church. A good story the preacher could have told was about Paul preaching until midnight. He was leaving the next morning, so he had a lot to say. Luke says the results of the long sermon was a boy sitting in a window on the third floor being preached to sleep. His name was Eutychus (Acts 20:7). He hit the ground like a rock. Paul ran down the stairs, lifted the boy and shouted, "He is alive!"

Funeral homes were thoughtful to pass out handheld fans at funerals. They were saved for relief at regular worship services. I tried not to look at the big letters or pictures on the fans. They cooled me, but did not lift my spirits. Today, we have mechanical miracles to help us keep cool at church. Usually we lock the thermostatic control box. It is hard to please everybody because we dress differently (spring, summer, fall, winter), all on the same summer day. Sometimes I get hot in my robe.

I have declined to have keys for drink machines and air conditioner control boxes. It is easier to just say, "Hey, you are cool!" That works for most everybody. Cool!

The Heart of the Ham

The smokehouse was the building where the butchered pork was sugar-cured, peppered, and stored. Suspended from rafters were: hams, shoulders, slabs of bacon, sacks of sausage and jowl. If someone could not sing hymns of praise coming from the smokehouse, they just didn't have the heart for singing. Whistlin' was just as good.

One of the familiar sights was a ham without a heart. Someone had taken a knife and cut out the hunk of meat in the form of a U between the bones. It was the heart of the ham. Usually, once during the winter that prize cut of country ham was delivered to the family doctor. It was a "thank offering" in appreciation of a loving and caring physician who had pulled a family through fractures, infections, colds, and fevers.

Money may pay debts, but it can never repay love, kindness, patience, commitment, forgiveness, and second-mile caring. Thanksgiving is our way of responding with the heart. We may not be able to symbolize it with the "heart of the ham", but we can express it some form of thanks---whether rejoicing, giving, or both.

Paul wrote, "Owe no one anything, except to love one another, for he who loves his neighbor has fulfilled the law." (Romans 13:8) Love is the one debt that never ends. Thanksgiving is a payment that is always appropriate, when it come from the heart. Happy Thanksliving!

The Town Character

Every community has "town characters". They are eccentric, often wonderfully simple people, and in many ways set a standard by which the community judges and is judged.

Pee Wee lived in a little country town. He was barely five feet tall and wore a wool army coat that swept the ground. He slept in the seed house at the cotton gin, and swept up the back at U-Tot-Em grocery. He ate boloney sandwiches, cheese and crackers, and drank Nehi Orange sodas as gifts or wages for odd jobs. Pee Wee gave everyone a sense of success. He fell through the "safety net".

Butter Bean carved for himself a little community in the big city. In the summer he lived on the Farmer's Market. Only God knows where he was in the winter. All the buyers of the big chain groceries knew Butter Bean, as well as farmers from Mississippi, Arkansas, and Tennessee. He could sleep under the trucks of friends from three states. When he wandered into the Market Restaurant at sunrise, a half dozen voices boomed, "Come on over Butter Bean, breakfast is on me." A big city can swallow up strangers, but Butter Bean gave credibility to the song, "Everybody like to go someplace, where everybody knows your name."

Marcelus made a place for himself in a County Seat town. He was the only man who wore goggles 365 days a year. He pushed a two-wheel cart filled with the tools of his trade: lawn mower, edger, hoe, hedge clippers, assorted blades for customized yard work. He was ingenious or "necessity was the mother of inventions" for he sat on a four legged stool mounted on wheels and pushed himself along as he trimmed the grass at the curb. He was one of the most dignified citizens of the community. Even in the heat of summer work, he wore a wide brimmed felt hat and a tie of some sort around his sweaty neck. Marcelus dressed as if he was fully convinced he was "made in the image of God." The greetings were simple, but profound. "Good morning, Marcelus." "Good morning to you." Thus the children of God communicated across their man-made fences.

A community is really in a mess without a "town character". How will one know what is up and what is down, or, what is straight and what is crooked? What is success? What is failure?

Thank you, Pee Wee. Thank you, Butter Bean. Thank you, Marcelus. Thank you, Lord. Yep, character is what it is all about—Town, Country, or Big City. Character! And, Caring!

Like a Three Ring Circus

When I was twelve years old, Daddy and Mother (Clark and Louise) took me and my brother, Billy, to the Circus at Madison County Fairgrounds in Jackson, Tennessee. Our neighbor, Guy Adams and his friend, Maureen Turner, went with us. The one thing I remember from the circus was an act with a clown and pig. The pig rode in a wheelbarrow the clown pushed. It slid down a washing board at rest stops. Mother used a washing board on Mondays, wash day, to do the weekly washing of clothes for our family. It was interesting to see a wash board could be used for fun.

Going to the circus became a family tradition for us when we were in Little Rock. I purchased twenty five tickets because the church bus had twenty five seats. We were always sold out. I will always remember Gunther Gebel Williams in the circus. He worked lions, tigers, horses and elephants. His children grew up traveling with the circus.

One year was called "The Big Tusk Show." One huge elephant had big tusks. Gunther rode the elephant around the three ring circus, standing and waving to the crowd because he was retiring soon from his position as trainer and ringmaster. The next year he wore dark coveralls, stood on the ground with the animals, and walked with them to and from the rings. His son, Mark, and daughter, Christina were center ring with the show. Gunther carried a broom and shovel, instead of a baton and whip. Gunther is my hero.

   "Ladies and Gentlemen, Children of All Ages, the Ringling Brother, Barnum and Bailey Circus is coming to Huntsville, Thursday November 29th, 7:00 p.m. We have purchased 50 tickets at $10.00 each. The sign up sheet is in the church office. First come is first served. We will leave the church parking lot at 6:00 p.m. Oh, I am not thinking about retirement. I am just changing rings. Sing with the ringmaster, "We will always have sparks in our eyes." Smile with grandson, Lorenzo, who says to grandfather, Gunther, "We are family...always." Sometimes life is like a three ring circus. Let the show begin.

The Crossin'

   One Saturday afternoon when I was a junior in high school I said "N____". I wish I could take it back, but it is history. We had gathered cucumbers on the farm and were washing, grading, and putting them in half a bushel baskets to haul to the Memphis Farmers Market Sunday afternoon for sales and distribution on Monday morning. Sarah, a faithful farm hand, sweet black lady and good friend was helping us. I was tired and irritated that we had to work late Saturday evening instead of going to town. I said, "I am ready to quit. It's n____ night." No one laughed, stared at me or rebuked me. I did all that to myself. In my heart I quietly resolved to never say that word out loud again.

N___ night was associated with the Crossin' at Humboldt. Two train tracks crossed. One from Memphis to Nashville, and one from Jackson to St. Louis. At the Crossin' were sheds where box cars and trucks could be loaded with cabbage, tomatoes, potatoes, cucumbers, bell peppers and other produce being shipped "up north." My first job was working for Mr. Dunlap. I graded tomatoes at the Crossin' and got my social security started. It was a real paycheck and the summer job helped a little bit on my sophomore year at Johnson Bible College. Mr. Dunlap trusted me. He sent three of us to Reelfoot Lake to load a truck with tomatoes. We went in a five ton truck. He asked me to drive. The other two guys were in their sixties. One had been tried for murder, and one hung out with beer. I enjoyed the guys and driving the truck. I got trusted at the Crossin'.

Saturday night was big and exciting for black people at the Crossin'. It was their town. On Saturday night, white folks just drove through the Crossin'. There were jive joints, and the music was loud. People laughed, talked, and had a blast—let down after a long work week. They shopped at the grocery story, drug store, Beare Ice and Coal Company, café and beer parlor. It was like a weekly homecoming as they greeted friends. Sometimes someone got a little wild with a knife, and the doctor was called back to his office. At the Crossin' I learned not to stare. The man in the jive door out-stared me. I learned God made a beautiful world. Look, listen, but don't waste time staring. Someone will be ready to stare you down.

"Po Tom"

Our barber had a shop at the Crossin'. He called himself "Po Tom". He had a little one-room shop across from his house on West Mitchell Avenue. Daddy would drop off my brother, Billy, and me to get a haircut. Daddy gave each of a quarter to pay Po Tom for the haircuts. He was a funny barber, humorous and friendly. Daddy could make a business stop while we got trimmed to look good at Sunday school and church. Looking good is another thing we learned at the Crossin'. Thanks to Po Tom.

One Easter Sunday, Kay's family was at church with a big crowd. Her little sister, Marsha Ann, was all dressed up pretty and was left with a crowd of children in the nursery. After church, parents came to get their children. But Marsha Ann had walked out with a chattering group of parents and children, and had walked down the street by herself. Kay's family was desperate to find her, driving around town searching. There she was, walking with a black man. Po Tom held her hand and was walking her back toward the church. She had walked all the way to the Crossin'. Thanks be to God for good people at the Crossin".

"And I, Barack Obama", on this 20th day of January, 2009, do sincerely affirm I will faithfully serve as President of the United States of America, at this Cross Roads of all the people, for the people, and by the people. So help me, God, in our transition, at the Crossing.

Seasons of the Holly Bush

The landscape artist chose the holly bush because of its potential. It took an eye of vision to choose a tiny bush seated quietly in a gallon bucket among the vast array of splendor in a spring greenhouse. Finally, when it was moved to the sun, it made shade and claimed its rightful place with spreading root and thorny leaf.

After a half dozen summer suns, the mockingbird came looking for a safe place to nest. Twigs, sticks, and strings were carefully arranged behind a wall of thick bush and briar into a cradle of legacy. Cheeps and peeps announced the scurry of coming and going with pierced quarry in beak. A creepy feline, scouting for dinner menu, approached the spiny wall of prickly leaves, and retreated empty-pawed. The holly fortress had been well chosen by some God-directed invisible imprint.

By fall, the green haven had mustered clusters of berries. Methodically, they turned from green to red, decorating a Christmas tree for creature and varmints of the wild. Again, the holly was chosen for table arrangements and brightening mantels by celebrants decking the halls. The bright red berries announced the joy of blessed birth and redemption of sacrifice. So the lowly holly hinted of the holy, chosen to spread Christmas joy.

The faithful holly bush kept its fading berries while winter's ice and snow held its grip. The birds came and went with the shift of the season. The key to migration was food, manna on the wing, daily bread, seed for the taking. A flock of Goldfinches descended without notice to the brightly berried holly bush. They flittered with growing appetites, seizing the harvest, feeding in frenzy and excitement. Suddenly, they were gone—and all the berries with them—together wedded in flight to a rhythm of next year. I heard no grace, but felt a welling doxology for God's wondrous mystery that ties generation to generation.

It is no accident the holly bush grows by home, path, mall, and sanctuary. It marks the seasons of our times—and His.

Chapter 4
Life Wish List

Life Wish List

The best life planners say we should be goal-oriented. It establishes direction, keeps motivation before us, and is a tool for evaluation. Motivators tell us to declare our goals for that helps us be accountable. Today, I will allow imagination to string a dozen.

- To minister this congregation toward its full, rich, and dynamic potential.
- To be there for our families, who have always been there for us.
- To build a tree house with our grandchildren.
- To travel the United States of America, and take time to look and listen.
- To write a book on memories from childhood called "Streaking on Sugar Creek".
- To serve as a consultant in helping congregations become active in bible study.
- To serve as minister in a large church, concentrating on pastoral calling in homes, hospitals, and nursing homes.
- To take hammer and saw, and help Habitat for Humanity build a house for poor persons.
- To own a pair of small mules, a wagon, a dog, a few plows, and a small plot of land.
- To grow vegetables, and invite gleaners into the fields to gather them free of charge.
- To pay all my debts.
- To love God and people, and to resist letting my circle get small.

Why the list? There is a wise saying, "He who aims at nothing usually hits it." I am aiming!

April 15—IRS, IRA and SRA

Becoming rich is possible by the discipline of making IRA investments during the forty years between twenty-five and sixty-five years of age. The key is acting on the maximum before the April 15th deadline.

It is a comfort to know one can prepare for the future spiritually. While there are not April 15 deadlines, we invest our lives with God day by day. . Church families are not like mushrooms. We grow in God's family through caring and sharing. We open our hearts to new members, and embrace all the church family. We keep our commitments (as best we can), and sacrifice personally, for the good of the whole. We may hope things will go our way, but we do not demand it.

The forty years between our adulthood and retirement should not be "wandering in the wilderness" years, but a deliberate spiritual journey toward a Promised Land...the security of material provisions and spiritual riches. Without both, we are not prepared to grow older or retire. A Spiritual Retirement Account (SRA) is an absolute for the Christian.

Paul writes in I Corinthians 13:13 "So faith, hope, love abide, these three; but the greatest of these is love."

In the end, our SRA is all that is left when the IRA is depleted and the IRS has forgotten us. Have you made a deposit of faith, hope and love in your SRA today?

America Past the Crossroads

Where will it lead us?—Michael, cosmic and vulgar; or Sarah, plain and tall? Two Sundays, a week apart, prime time. One song and dance for the backroom bar, and one for the living room. Children on the floor for both. The children of the world saw it all, in their name. What's wrong in the school? What is wrong in the mall. What's wrong on the streets? A sewer of cable and cassette, leaks relentlessly on the floor of the living rooms, at the children's feet. At $28,000 a second, can it ever be stopped? God bless you, "Sarah, Plain and Tall". Take your place in America and weep in the school yards. Flush, flush: Flow, flow! Pretty minds, beautiful children, robbed of innocence, thrust prematurely into the adult world where tender innocence was buried on Boot Hill with Hopalong Cassidy. Hello, Sarah. Hello, Skylark. When will we see you again? Hurry back! Anne of Green Gables wants your autograph, too.

Detours on the Christmas Journey

Scripture: "Thus there were fourteen generations in all from Abraham to David, fourteen from David to the exile to Babylon, and fourteen from the exile to Christ." Matthew 1:18

The first Christmas came after dust of many roads, decades of travel, and difficult detours. Luke begins the story of the birth of Christ by emphasizing that the road to Christmas was long, hard, and consisted of generations of pilgrims of faith who passed the baton over the centuries. Luke writes of three stages in the blessed hope come to pass: "fourteen generations from Abraham to David, fourteen generations from David to the exile in Babylon, and fourteen generations from the exile to Christ." When the people of Israel were slaves in exile and struggled to "sing the Lord's song in a strange land" many must have doubted that God would fulfill his promise to the ancient patriarch, "your seed shall be as many as the sands of the sea and stars of heaven, and by your family all the families of the earth will be blessed."

At one time or another, all of us will feel exiled along the road to Christmas. Not everyone can fulfill the dreaming song, "I'll be home for Christmas." A grandparent is no longer able to travel, and they tend the home fires alone while the younger generation travels to another town, city, or state. A doctor is on call Christmas Eve and must leave the family reunion and dinner to sew gunshot wounds or set broken bones. A police officer calls home on Christmas day to explain that his shift has been lengthened to do paperwork from the investigation of families out of control. Someone has a first Christmas alone, bereaved, floating on a sea of memories, whose time is fed by their own tears. "Home Alone" is more than a movie of survival entertainment. Everyone will taste the bitterness of exile on the journey to Christmas. Thank God, Christmas may find us lonely, but never alone. God has given us his Christmas gift of the presence of Christ. Exile is not the destination, but a detour between promise to Abraham and fulfillment in Jesus.

Prayer: Dear God, help me to believe and trust you in my lonely times of exile. May I be a helpful presence to others delayed by life's detours on the Christmas road.

Rome Past the Crossroads

The populace, 400,000 strong, greeted the warriors. Chariots rolled toward the marketplace, and vanity was rampant. The crowd was so spirited in the win that some fought among themselves. It was reported that violence even reached women in the villas. The city forum cleaned up the debris with weak apology for the populace, but applause for the gladiators, their captains, and generals. Two weeks of basking in glory. Shadowy visitation of seven deadly apparitions, each underestimating the price of the giant pig bladder. Basking in the glow of contracts.

In another province, some 5,000 citizens gathered around the pall of another champion. He died in battle with an invisible enemy which threatened every man, woman, and child of the empires of the world. He was crowned King Arthur at the Wimbledon. In victory, he did not publicly humiliate his defeated enemy with preening and strutting. He did not hold out his winning racket to taunt his worthy opponent. Instead, he used his energy to love his family, support his friends, and help the ill.
"Friends, Romans, countrymen, lend me your ears;
   I come to bury Caesar, not to praise him.
   The evil that men do lives on after them;
   The good is often interred with their bones.
     So let is be with Caesar."

There is a lasting glory that follows the memory of a gentleman, even if he happens to be a champion. Wait up, Spartacus and El Cid, for Arthur.

Thank God and McDonald's

In the Lord's Prayer, we pray, "Give us this day our daily bread." The meaning of that prayer for us individually is somewhere between one good hot meal a day, and a lifestyle in the manner to which we have become accustomed.

For a mother in Ethiopia, it means a cup of milk and a bowl of gruel for her hollow-eyed child, and perhaps herself. For the homemakers, it may mean peanut butter sandwiches, laced with red, white or blue jelly around April 15. On an Interstate between Kansas City and St. Louis, a truck driver has a Big Mac attack, and prayerfully scans the horizons for the oasis of the golden arch.

The breaking of bread is as old as hunger. It's forms have taken new shapes. Retirees swarm around tables at McDonald's for Sunday morning breakfast. Children rearrange the backseats of compacts as they break into their "happy meal boxes". Pizza is delivered to the door, guaranteed hot. A fling to Adam's Rib on the weekend for prime rib or seafood breaks the monotony of quick fix. Others stand in line for food stamps.

When we ask God for daily bread, are we asking for needs or wants, necessities or the manner of lifestyles to which we have become accustomed?

Luke 22:19 says, "Jesus took bread and when he had given thanks, he broke it and gave it to them and said, 'This is my body given for you.'" It was in the breaking and sharing of bread that they were fed.

As the poet has said, "The songs we sang were more than songs. The bread we broke was more than bread."

See you at the Lord's Table Sunday.

The Cooing of a Turtle Dove

When I was a "little rascal" on the way from the barn to Sugar Creek, I experienced a "loss of childhood innocence." The Daisy BB gun I got for Christmas was nearly always in my hand. There was a turtle dove sitting on a nest in a Catalpa (Tawby) tree. I aimed but something happened inside of me. I could not pull the trigger. I still shot mules, frogs, and snakes. But not turtle doves.

A few weeks ago at Sunday Worship we were having a quiet personal prayer time. In the silence I heard the cooing of a turtle dove. It brought back a flood of memories. Hiram was on our trip to Israel in 1994. We came to the Jordan River. Without words, we all slowed down and were in deep thought as we came up to the banks of the Jordan. Hiram asked one of his young minister friends to baptize him in the Jordan. I said, "Hiram, you are a minister. Why do you want to be baptized in the Jordan. You were baptized years ago and have done many baptisms." He said, "I want to be baptized where Jesus was baptized." We quietly watched. When he was raised out of the water, I heard the cooing of a turtle dove.

Luke describes Jesus' baptism this way: "Jesus was baptized, the heavens were opened, a voice said,

'You are my beloved Son in whom I am well please,' and the Holy Spirit descended in a bodily shape like a dove."(Luke 3:21-22) At the bird feeder in the back yard, the doves gather. They never light on the feeder. They walk quietly and pick up fallen grain. When they land, they flutter and settle down gently. Sometimes at dusk, in the last traces of daylight, they fly like arrows to the roosting place to coo for the moonlight and peaceful night.

When the doves coo, I pray, "And the voice of the turtle dove was heard in the land." Stop! Look! Listen! Do you hear it? No, not a train. A dove. Yes, I hear it. Thank you, Jesus.

Gain the Best from the Test

When little is required, little is gained. One of the worst things that can happen to us is never to face trials and tribulations. As the body builders say, "No pain, no gain." The final exam forces us to recall, relate, and finally, renounce or rejoice.

Jesus faced the testing of Passion Week. He was publicly accused, spent a long prayerful night on the Mount of Olives, while his disciples slept from exhaustion, and faced the cruelty of the cross. But in it all, he gave us the Lord's Supper as a memorial, the courage of his faith in the face of suffering, the example of his grace in forgiving ignorance, and the joyful resurrection of hope.

The challenges of life call for new strength, courage, and greater effort. Each new victory is a stepping stone to greater faith in God.

James says, "Count it all joy, my brethren, when you meet various trials, for you know that the testing of your faith produces steadfastness." (James 1:2)

News Release
Love is...being there.

One thing I have learned from both my family and church family-- love means being there. When it comes to making judgments about the church, most everyone believes he is an expert. Even a novice, at a casual glance or a halfhearted participant in worship, believes he can see more through a keyhole than saints will ever see through an open door. As a 40 year old veteran, there is much I do not know about the church; but I am an expert on how well the church loves—for I have been blessed by its steadfast love.

You were there when we were children, teaching us the songs of faith and self worth. You sent us to camp and conference where we learned the meaning of morning watch, prayer, and Christian fellowship. You organized trips, bought us bus tickets and paid taxi fares to help us fill our teenage cups with "the taste of new wine". You gave us true values in a world that spent billions trying to get our attention.

You were there holding wide the door when we made a decision about our life's work. You opened a college and two seminaries to us. You paid our tuition more than once. You gave us skilled teachers of deep personal faith who opened to us the treasure of the scripture. You gave us gifts that kept us going.

You were there in giving your blessing to our marriage. You were there when each of the children was born. You babysat, brought food, and just plain "helped". You taught our children as you had taught us. You were there when they were baptized, and you have been there when they married.

You have encouraged us when we were weak. You have forgiven us when we failed. You never allowed us to settle for too little. You have been with us in sickness and death. Anytime, every time, and all the time we look up and "you are there".

There will always be pettiness about squeaky doors and stubby brooms, mere lightning bugs in the presence of your beautiful love and light. You are the church, God's creation, and we love you. Thank you for always being there. You are God's people.

John says, "Behold, the dwelling of God is with men. He will dwell with them, and they shall be his peoples, and God himself will be with them." (Revelation 21:3)

Who is Boo Radley?

Who is Boo Radley? The name hangs in my mind like a dirt dauber's nest on a barn wall. It is there with a story encased. Something special is hunkered down for a flight into human hearts. There is a treasure to be opened. A celebration is to be planned. There will be a party to remember a scrimmage line that did not deter a touchdown, a deed that opened a door to a better tomorrow, and a compassion that put a haunting terror to rest. Who is Boo Radley?

Was he a "Big Apple Rapper?
> I am Boo Diddle Whopper, Just tryin' to popper, see me cast my net.
> Just hoppin' the ground, looking around, to see what I've found.
> Up beside me is a fine little kitten, just wantin' a little scratch.
> Better pickin's than a watermelon patch, in an asphalt jungle by wall street hatch.
> Could ole Boo jive and shake a booty good, hang down jeans where ankles stood?
> The Boo I'm thinkin' is not a rapper, he is too good to be a lapper or a crapper.

Was Boo Radley a quarterback on a football field? The fellers in the barber shop were talking about "Big Bad Boo." He made history on the football field, a famous quarter back. He was the master of gaining yardage. He could throw a pass so fast the opposition was still hearing the count. He was rare on rendering interceptions. He could pass that ball to the full back so quick it did not stick in the big bubba defense line. Boo became a legend. When trucks pass with windows down, you hear guys talking about Boo. Even girls getting their hair fixed on Saturday chat about Boo. There is talk of Boo's picture coming out on a Pepsi can. What a blast! THE BAMA BOO BURP!

Oh, now I know. The Boo Radley I remember is in Harper Lee's <u>To Kill a Mockingbird</u>, a story of compassion and caring by an author from Alabama. The story is about a lawyer defending a black man being accused and tried for rape. The lawyers little girl is Scout and his little boy is named Jim. They are taught respect by a black pastor in the balcony of the court house where the children are sitting, and he asked them to stand with him in respect for their father. "Stand up Miss Scout. Your father is passing." But Boo was a good neighbor and friend. He was mentally challenged, but tender hearted. He left a pocket knife in a hole in a post for Jim, who checked every day as he, boy-like, looked for treasure. Boo was in the woods on Halloween and saved Scout from a wicked man who vengefully wanted to turn spooking to assault. In the end, Boo Radley sat in the swing, not just mentally challenged but mentally challenging every reader. Do the right thing, even at wrong times. Who is Boo Radley? My hero!

Chapter 5
From June Bugs to Transformers

From June Bugs to Transformers

From Christmas to New Year's there is ample opportunity to watch children at play. They go about their business of practicing for adulthood while the parents and grandparents debate the issues of toys—too many, too expensive, too violent, too weird, etc.

Overcome with nostalgia, they talk of making their own toys. They made tractors of spools and rubber bands, matchsticks, and buttons. Extra traction was added by notching the spool. There is reminiscing about warm summer days when June bugs were captured, flown in circles by strings or hitched as a team to penny match boxes. The virtue of creating and making play things is applauded.

When Transformer toys were first mentioned, the mind raced over memories of train sets and slot car racers. Soon it was obvious that Transformer toys were different from Tinker Toys, Erector Sets, and Legos. It is the age of Masters of the Universe, Robots, Hulk Hogan, R2D2, and Triple Transformers—from tank, to plane, to robot, and back.

Transformer toys have invaded the house with a horde of plastic people, insects, crawlers, changing shapes and sizes, gathering up an array of cars, tanks, claws and swords into a full bodied defender of good. The scenario is directed by five year olds who have barely learned to tie their shoes.

An "expert" on children and toys recently said, "Children love Transformer toys because they are in control." They can shape and reshape by exerting control over the make-believe world. They become Masters of the Universe, and in vivid imagination, reshape the outcome of make-believe.

Let the little people play and practice the battles of good and evil. They are practicing for the day they will be in control. Maybe they can learn to do it better. It may be a long way from June bugs to Transformers, but the game is still the same—practicing for tomorrow.

There is no greater power available for reshaping our lives than the gift of God's Son. He reshapes the person as focused in Romans 12:2, "Do not be conformed to this world, but be transformed by the renewal of your mind, that you may prove what is the will of God, what is good and acceptable and perfect." A needy world will never outlive its hunger for the fodder of Bethlehem's manger. Christ is still the Master of the triple change---heart, habit, and hope. Happy New Year!

A Feast of Memories

Families across the land gather on this Thanksgiving Day,
To count God's many blessings along life's winding way.
Their tables burdened with turkey, sweet potatoes, and Cranberries,
Are small compared to your banquet of a feast of memories.
> Fifty golden years of love and marriage,
> Kisses and dreams, hard work, and baby carriage.

Little girl fleeing from a black snake in the pasture,
And little boy spurring his pony to go faster.
Along the field roads they sneak,
Peeking at each other over Sugar Creek.
    Both entwined by romance and joy,
    Becoming the miracle of girl and boy.

Catch a chicken to become a preacher's fare,
And bring some eggs for change to spare.
What an appetite after saying "I do,"
Buy some cheese and crackers for the first chew.
    Some cannot whistle while eating crackers,
    But you were not afraid it would hinder your smackers.

First born, warming at the kitchen stove, with deliberate muse,
Contemplating how to bake Mother's shoes.
Second born labor, with neighbor so nice,
Drinking your lemonade and eating the ice.
    The beginnings of little troubles and big joys,
    Creek, pond, river, snake in a can, and two little boys.

The land spread out somehow between the bank and God,
To be the cradle of lovers who turn the sod.
A faithful caravan of teams—Joe and Blue, Red and Maude and Charlie,
Rows of cotton and corn, cabbage and tomatoes, but not barley,
    Cabbage sprouts for the market and leaving at five.
    "Hurry up, boys, we ought to be at the four-way drive."

There is much to be achieved in the course of one's life,
But what lasting joys for one husband and wife.
Mother and Daddy, how do you so gracefully hold fifty years of love,
And be host to a million memories on earth and above?
    We congratulate you on your success.
    For at the crossroads, you chose the best.

Now, we honor you for what you have done but there is still much to do,
For lovers do not stop loving, and there are grandchildren, too.
Who will fill our freezers and applaud when the children perform?
We need you to help keep our love warm.
    Your golden wedding anniversary makes you a sage,
    We are counting on you to help us not miss a page.

50 Years celebrated on November 22, 1979

November 22, 1929
Mary Louse Patterson Stegall
William Clark Stegall, Sr.

Instant, Home-Grown, or Both?

    I love potatoes in all shapes, forms, and fashions. Two weeks ago, I planted seed potatoes in the backyard garden. I look at the barren rows daily—not a sign of life. Over their hidden secrets, I utter a green-thumb prayer, "Come on, potatoes! Do your thing. May the Lord bless you real good!"

While I wait, I think. An instant potato mentality can sure confuse you in the presence of the real thing. I can microwave an Idaho monster in five minutes, including a pat of butter and crown of sour cream. And instant mashed potatoes are as near as the whistle on a teakettle. In a supermarket world I muse, "How can seed potatoes be so slow when their offspring are so fast?"

Perhaps the lesson is that the garden and supermarket are parent and child, separated by time and distance. One nurtures patience, and the other instant gratification—the latter humbled to the first at the long checkout line. Time is the gift of God, and patience, the steady stride toward a bountiful harvest and daily bread.

Paul says, "But if we hope for what we do not see, we wait for it with patience." (Romans 8:25)

While we wait, let's rehearse the doxology for a warm sun shining on God's good earth.

Aaron's Chariot

In the book of old, for you,
It is told of a man named Jehu.
He was charged to make things right with Jezebel
For the future depended on him to right wrongs
    for Israel.

He was in a hurry to do what was right,
So he rushed to his chariot with all his might.
He took his mission very seriously,

And in tribute his biographers said, "Jehu driveth
    furiously."

He did not have the advantage of four on the floor,
Or, five speeds between bucket seats to give him
    more.
He trusted in the Lord and two wild mustangs
To speed him on his mission with the agility of
    orangutans.

He was a faithful servant in his task,
That the Lord told the prophet to take up the flask.
For his victory all Israel would sing,
And by the word of the Lord Jehu was anointed King.

In the book of new for everyone,
It is told of a man named Aaron.
Who was charged to things right for Agnes and the
    girls,
For everyone depended on him to do things in whirls.

He was in the mood to do what was right,
So he rushed to his chariot with all his might.
He yanked open the door and climbed on to the seat,
Brushing aside coffee cups and dog hair—making
    things neat.

He bridled the Olds 88 into reverse.
And it moaned, groaned, and roared back with a burst.
With a touch of his foot the horses leaped forward,
With octane and affection as their only reward.

He delivered one to music lessons,
Then on to Food World and the delicatessen.
Stop by the church to check on a light,

Wheel up to Lexington and get back by night.
Only by the long strides of his steeds would he make the Masonic meeting,
But he had time to pick up two rainbows by the time they were seating.
Perhaps there is time to fetch the chainsaw for the farm,
Then, on to Reynolds to pull the graveyard without due alarm.
The Pinto and the Buick are not exactly a modern disgrace,
But, it is with the faithful Olds 88 that Aaron saves face.
Sometimes it requires a drive like Aaron, the priest,
Or the angel, Michael, to bring out the beast.

So, here is our tribute to our Aaron Michael, Faithful, fast, diligent, and loyal.
"And the driving is like the driving of Jehu, the son of Nimshi; for he drives furiously." (II Kings 9:20b)

Pairs and Spares Christmas Party
    December 20, 1980

A Creamy Tribute

Woody, do you recall your childhood days,
When you were a boy in a million ways?

Whether you rose early or late,
At the barn you had a date--- with Bess.

A pail for the milk and boots for the slush,
Away you hurried in a hungry rush.

A few nubbins from the crib, and shucks for the fodder,
You steadied ole Bess to become a squatter.

Seated on stool with head in her flank,
You boldly laid two hands on her tank.

Dashing warm water from the pail,
To her back leg securing her tail.

Her fly swatter was no disgrace,
But who wants a swat in the face?

Warm water on a cold morn reduces her shudder,
Many cannot milk, but none can milk butter.

Two hands and four spigots is not so rare,
Two for the work, and two for the spare.

The bucket filled with snow-white treasure,
Just a pause to squirt the cat with pleasure.

Thank you, Bess! With a slap on her back,
Off of my toe, please, or your head I will crack.

Woody, do you recall those childhood days,
When you were a boy in a million ways.

Thank you, God, for food on the table,
Thank you, Bess—willing and able.

This tribute to Bess is more than a fable,
Some of life's best men have passed through the stable.

Here is a portrait for your den wall.
Bess is number one—but you are best of all.

Tribute to Woody
Presented at the Pairs and Spares Christmas Party in
Florence, Alabama
December 18, 1973

Dear Friend

Dear Friend,

    When she gave her offering, I knew she was living on a small Social Security check. No doubt it was because she was a good manager that she was always able to bring an offering. When the plate was passed, it never caught her empty handed. The offering never sent her into a deep spiritual experience where the passing plate came as an interruption in her walk with God. Instead, she faced the plate head on--- eyes up---with a smile on her face. As I watched her anticipate the thrill of bringing her gift, I thought of the scripture in Deuteronomy 16:16, "They shall not appear before the Lord empty handed; every man shall give as he is able, according to the blessings of the Lord, your God, which he has given you."

    The worst part of me wanted to interrupt her joy. Dear Lady, the scripture says "every man", so why not leave the work of the church to the men? And how is it that you have managed to bring an offering every Sunday from so little, when others with so much are pressed to find both the means and the motivation? And for my final shot---your weekly sacrifice helped pay for the soft cushion your prosperous neighbor enjoys rent-free. Yet my devilish ploy was only met with the same gentle smile I regularly saw radiating over the collection plate. Strange thing about that lady, year in and year out she never came before the Lord empty handed, and going and coming I never saw her when her hands were empty. She was a living witness to "the blessings of the Lord." My dear friend, do you think cameras in the ceiling would make as much difference as mirrors in the offering plate?

Affectionately,
Caleb

Covering Arrears

Dear Friend,

Thank you for the scripture reference, "But you shall receive power when the Holy Spirit has come upon you; and you shall be my witnesses in Jerusalem and all Judea and Samaria, and to the end of the earth." (Acts 1:8) It helped me make a decision at church. Also, the minister asked me to be in charge of Public Relations.

I have always wanted to be a PR person, so I leapt at the opportunity. You know, we really have something to sell the public... a church that is nearly 2,000 years old and devoted to serving God by helping people. We have story after story of how lives have been changed by the love of God. I have completed several interviews with people in our congregation who have consented to sharing their testimony. Appointments have been made with the TV station, newspaper, radio, billboard ads, and the college paper for next week.

But, Sunday the Chairman of the Board dropped a bomb on me. He said, "Our church is in arrears." Now, how in heaven's name can I be a PR man for the church when it is in arrears? Would this caption fit: "Come to the church of the arrears"? I am challenged by representing a church that is up front—nice building, pretty lawn, floodlights at night, bills paid, friendly people, serving the community, evangelistic, cushions on the pews. But as attractive as we make the church from front to back, people still prefer to sit in arrears. We park our cars arrears. We pledge arrears. And our primary entrance is in arrears.

Brother, you can see my dilemma. The minister says we need to do something about our image. The Chairman of the Board says we must do something about our arrears. Can you make any thing large enough to cover arrears?

Your desperate PR friend,
Caleb

Hail Joseph, Full of Commitment

I have never seen a living nativity scene without Joseph at the shoulder of Mary, and the two behind the Christ child in the manger. It may be true to life but that makes it no less a true ideal. Joseph is a male role model of love and commitment.

One of the casualties of culture is the non-committal male. U.S. News, in a recent article, stated that one out of four babies is born out of wedlock in the U.S. The News Channel recently said one in four unwed mothers marry before the birth of the child. Hail Joseph, full of commitment.

"Out of Africa", one of my favorite stories, showcases the poverty of the noncommittal male. Karen and Brawd go to Africa under the umbrella of marriage to find fortune. Brawd takes her wealth and gives her venereal disease in return. Denys moves in and fills the void with classical music, safaris in the bush, and an airplane view of the beauty of Africa's abundant wildlife. The one thing she asks of him he denies her, to share his name. She returns to her native land—broke, alone, full of memories, and the wiser.

One of the most insightful books I have read this year is <u>Iron John</u>—a book about men, by Robert Bly. He says the images of adult manhood given by popular culture are worn out. He would take us back to the stories of hearth and fairy tales that move a boy from the mother's realm to the father's realm. He says there is a grief in men, a brokenness that emerges from the void left by the absent father.

Thank God for the story of all the stories--- Mary and Joseph, and a child lying in a manger. Hail Joseph—carpenter, builder, taxpayer, traveler, refugee, lover, host of angels, host of heaven's bread. Stand tall, Joseph---masculine, caring, responsible, tearful at heaven's beauty. The wounded men of the world are looking for a model, a mentor, a second father or a second king.

The scent of heaven's bread rides on the four winds to the four corners. Hail Jesus---counselor, King of Kings, Prince of Peace. Hail Mary---full of grace. Hail Joseph, full of commitment.

Wise men still come to the manger of Bethlehem. There we find role models of commitment that ultimately lead us to the prayer of arrival, "Our Father in heaven..."

The Perfect Gift

The search is on for the perfect gift. It has to be something with class, useful, and representing a mountain of love. It is somewhere within the Christmas Triangle of the Mall, Uncle Charlie's (Flea Market), and Downtown. It is well within the reach and means of all.

A designer gift seems just perfect as far as class. When anyone sees the brand, they know it is the perfect combination of craftsmanship and machine, with the process being carefully purified by a revolving charge account. The only problem with a designer belt is that one must wear the coat open to display the buckle. That's weird in winter.

Blue Heel is the crown of the phrase "brand new" to those old timers whose first shirts were size 4-8-8 from the stencil on a fertilizer or feed sack. Blue Heel is the passport from famine to feast. The only problem with Blue Heel socks is one has to roll up the pant legs to show off the logo, and then someone thinks you are wearing "high waters." That's gross.

Uncle Charlie's (Flea Market) offers options galore, all the way from the new and the worn, the unsold or the unwanted, the unredeemed and the unredeemable. How about a unique saucer-sized belt buckle engraved with a rodeo cowboy riding a 2,000 pound Brahma bull, being hazed by thirteen colorfully dressed rodeo clowns. The problem results in searching for a heavy-duty pair of rainbow suspenders to hold up the western scenario.

The search narrows within the triangle—something classy, useful and loving, with the reach and means of all. The perfect gift is Time.
- --have lunch together sometime
- --find time to make a phone call
- --make time to write a letter
- --take time for a visit
- --devote 30 minutes to listening
- --lend some time to tossing a ball
- --invite someone on a drive to see the Christmas lights
- --attend worship with family and friends

The Wise Men first gave their time to search for "he who was born King of the Jews. For we have seen his star in the East and have come to worship him." (Matthew 2:2)

Strange that we have so little time, when it's the best gift of all. To give time is to give your self. Can you spare a time, brother?

A Concrete Ode to John Coleman
By: A. Busy Body

John is a whiz in the kitchen.
Especially if it's food he's a-fixin'.
When he is tossin' a salad called "chef"
He adds everything himself.
He will really stir up your affection
When he serves you his baked confection.

He is the king of coffee at the church.
If he is available to brew, we don't search.
Anyone can add salt and coffee to water,
But John adds them in the exact order.
He holds the gold cup for his part,
"The master of the brewer's art."

At Stylon he is first in the file.
He is the chief engineer of ceramic tile.
Millions of bare feet stand on his work.
Some folks bathe behind it without a smirk.
He has proportionately mixed clay and silica sand
To produce a tile—the best in the land.

Pouring his driveway is a different story.
Poor calculations rob him of his glory.
How can a man get so much right,
And for one little error wait all night.
It is the old story of war—man, horse, shoe, nail.
So close to victory, so near to fail.

But we are proud of you, John, though a
    wheelbarrow short,
A man who does so much right has no cause to
    snort.

Here is your very own concrete truck.
No more waiting for just a little dab of muck.
My friend, may it remind you not to be sad,
You are tops, and three out of four ain't bad.

Presented at the Pairs and Spares Christmas Party at Bonanza Steak House in 1974.

Chapter 6
You Got the Bama Buzzard

You Got the Bama Buzzard

On a trip back home for Thanksgiving one of the children asked, "Daddy, is that a hawk or a buzzard?" While driving our 1959 Ford, I would hold up one hand (well, we drive while holding a cell phone) and spread out my fingers. See that buzzard up there? The feathers on the ends of its wings are spread out like my fingers are spread. The hawk keeps its feathers tight. The hawk flaps its wings and the buzzard soars. Check out the wings and you will know if it is a buzzard.

For three and one half years I commuted to Lexington Theological Seminary (1974-1977) for over 300 miles one way. I bought a Citizen's Band Radio to keep in touch on trips. Drivers used all kinds of "handles": Hot Tator, Bubba One, Big Wheeler, Apple Dumplin', etc. Sometimes they used the same call names. I wanted to use a personal, down home, different name. Since I loved to watch buzzards soar, I said, "You got 'The Bama Buzzard' here." I didn't have to worry about somebody stealing "my handle".

A dear friend from 1969 in Florence was traveling with me to a Regional Assembly in South Alabama. I got on my Citizen's Band Radio for a chat and signed off, "Bama Buzzard, ten four." She quickly replied, "I am NOT going to call you "Bama Buzzard." To her last day on this earth she called me "Brother Bob." I pass a place over in Moulton I call "Buzzard Roost." I think it is the cow pasture more than the tall trees. Maybe it's both. People are always asking, "What do you want us to call you?' I am always just thankful to be called. Preacher. Young Man. Feller. Interim. Intern. Brother Bob, Robert, Bobby, etc. May the buzzards soar forever.

Good News at the Marketplace

"And there is danger not only that this trade of ours may come to disrepute but also the temple of the great goddess Artemis may count for nothing..." (Acts 19:27a)

The Gospel in Conflict

When Paul preached the good news of Gods' love in Christ, the result was often conflict. He traveled as a good citizen and wanted to be a good Roman citizen. Yet, the good news was sometimes in conflict with the businesses of some of the cities he visited, which resulted in political and economic unrest.

Personally, I love the ways of peace and like to emphasize that Jesus taught, "Blessed are the peacemakers for they will be called the sons of God." (Matthew 5:9) But He also calls us to an ultimate loyalty in His prayer, "Thy kingdom come, thy will be done, on earth as it is in heaven." (Matthew 6:10) Perhaps, there are times when being faithful to the Prince of Peace means conflict among princes of prosperity.

We still hold much in common with Paul's time and world, and hopefully the same gospel. The Ephesians were angry that "Paul had persuaded many that gods made with hands are not gods." (Acts 19:26b) They feared a depressed economy. Their fear nearly resulted in a riot.

I think it is important for us to remember again that change is inevitable in politics, religion, and the economy. But the calling of our Lord is not to make the politics or the economy our ultimate loyalty. Jesus Christ is Lord. And because He is Lord, we will always be interested in politics and economy. His Lordship must be remembered where laws are made, interpreted, and enforced. And I cannot believe that He is disinterested in the marketplace where money is earned and spent. It will be a sad day for Christian faith and the world when the gospel does not dare call the values of the world into question, and Christians are contend to be comforted.

What Not To Do

    Guy and Bess were neighbors. They were like an uncle and aunt. They lived on a twenty-acre farm that was the source of all their income. They had a dog, Victor, and he and I never became friends. He didn't want a friend, and I had plenty of dog friends at home. One day Bess came over to the yard and said, "Bobby, my cow got out of the pasture. Will you help me find her and bring her back?" I was honored by her invitation and trust. I found the cow grazing along our road to Sugar Creek. I led her back and returned her to the pasture. Bess was so relieved to have their milk cow back home. She gave me a dime with a big "Thank you, Bobby." I gave the dime back and suggested she use it to purchase a better wire fence so the cow would not get out again. It haunts me to think of what I proudly said to this humble and kind neighbor. If I could go back I would say, "Thank you Bess. How thoughtful of you. I am going to buy a coke and bag of peanuts at Mullins' Grocery."

Sarah, Ava, and Bess were black women who worked on the farm for day wages. It helped them buy salt, pepper, sugar, flour, meal and aspirin. Daddy gave me the job of working with them choppin' cotton. He said I was to "lead the hands." That meant I was to stay up front, not follow. When someone got behind, maybe a little more Johnson Grass on their row, then I went back and helped them catch up and stay with the group. We never wanted anyone to fall behind and not able to be part of the working group. One day Sarah told the story of when she was a little girl. She shared how her Daddy gave her peas to plant in the garden. She wanted to play. After awhile she realized her Dad was coming to check on her. In haste she dropped all the peas in a posthole and pulled dirt over them. She reported to her father she had finished planting. In two weeks there were no peas in the garden, but pea vines covered the ground around the post. I learned from Sarah that today's work will show up tomorrow. Even bold claims can be challenged by lousy results.

Sugar Creek sometimes flooded after heavy rains. Trees and bushes flourished on the banks of the creek over the years. The government sent a crew with a dragline to clear out the overgrown and often flooding Sugar Creek. I loved to go and watch the workmen. One man was on the dragline, tossing and pulling the bucket filled with sand and dirt. He dumped it on the banks and they grew higher with each dump. The creek became deeper and wider making a good flow of water to the Forked Deer River. The second man was a mechanic and maintenance worker who greased, cleaned, repaired and kept the big machine working. The men were challenged by huge trees. They cut the trees and used explosives to blow up the stumps.

One day I went down to the creek to watch them. I found a foot-long stick of something. I picked it up and tossed it around in my hands while I watched them work. I heard a voice speaking softly, "Son, lay that down gently. You found a stick of dynamite that did not go off." Sometimes we pick up more than we need to handle. Be safe. Listen to the wisdom of the experienced.

    Homework was going home from school in the afternoon to do the daily chores on the farm. Go to the barn and throw hay out of the barn loft for the mules. Shuck some corn for the pigs. Cover the tomato plant beds with the cotton sheet and add some broom straw to the top because the radio said there would be a frost tonight. Bring some coal in for the stove in the living room. Study time for me was during library time at school. I am sure I could have made better grades if I had studied at home, but averaging B's meant I had potential with more concentration on book work. Doing the chores in the evening was a learning experience. Milking the cow was one of my jobs. Take a pail of water to wash the udders so there will be no dark dots on the milk. Feed the cow to keep her still. Pull up a box to sit on at her flank. Aim at the bucket. Hit the target. Flies were often real pests. They buzzed on the cow and on me. She swished her tail in defense. The cow's tail was her homegrown flyswatter. But, she swatted me over and over again. In defense I parted the long hair at the end of her tail and tied it around her leg. Good job. She can't swat me. The next evening Daddy said, "Bobby, when I went to milk ole Bess this morning her tail was tied to her leg. Did you do that last night?" "Yes sir, I did. She kept swatting me when she was after the flies," I replied. Daddy made the point with the question of accountability. Ole Bess could not use nature's defense mechanism for 12 hours against her attackers. Sometimes a little accommodating plan can mess up a bigger and better plan.

Vocational Agriculture was a favorite study, and I had career thoughts in mind. I took the class for four years in High School. It also opened the door for FFA (Future Farmers of America). I served as treasurer. We made many trips for judging cattle and pigs, and Billy and I attended a week of camp one summer. One day trip was near Dyer, Tennessee. I had received my driver's license and offered to drive the family car. Mr. Shankle said that would be fine. He said, "Follow me." After our observations and lessons at the cattle ranch he said, "Boys, I am driving over to see my Mom and Dad. They live just a little ways down the road. Be safe driving back to school." We headed back to Humboldt. Franklin, Lehman, Jerry and E.L, were with me. Someone said, "Let's turn on the gravel road that goes by Franklin's house. It is a nice little drive and Mr. Shankle is going by to see his Mom and Dad." Sure. Good idea. We will beat him back to school. It was a short detour, but Mr. Shankle was at school waiting for us. He said, "Bobby, why are you late?" I said, "We drove by Franklin's house." Suggestions can come from many people, even good trustworthy friends. The one driving is responsible for remembering the Master Plan. There are goals, destinations, and detours. Listen up!

They say college is a four- year experience that offers the opportunity to find out who you are and where you are headed. That is true in my experience. I learned to live away from home, being responsible for my room, clothing, money, work, assignments, travel, friends, career, etc. I was Bobby when I left home. Mrs. Bourne called me "Mr. Stegall." She was letting me and my classmates know she was expecting the best from her class. She taught Prose and Poetry. We had to write papers every week. One Thanksgiving, I returned to Humboldt for a long weekend. I went to Central Avenue Christian Church and heard Mr. Bill Huie preach. While listening to his great sermon and delivery I began writing my paper for Mrs. Bourne, due the week of my return to College. It began like his sermon from Hebrews 1:1, "God, who in sundry times and divers manners spake in time past unto the fathers by the prophets..." I followed this pattern of writing in my paper. Mrs. Bourne called me to her desk after class and said, "Mr. Stegall, this does not sound like you. Where did you get it?" I said, "From my pastor, Brother Huie. I heard him preach this last weekend when I was home for Thanksgiving weekend." Mrs. Bourne said, "Mr. Stegall, be yourself. God wants to use you and your gifts in ministry. Be Yourself."

Traveling John came through our community once a year for several years. He carried a leather pack on his shoulders, filled with handy and helpful things you could purchase. I never saw him drive a car or a truck. He walked. I often wondered as a little boy if he spent the night under bridge over Sugar Creek. He was small, strong, and had a strange accent when he spoke. I think he was from St. Louis, Missouri, but I don't have any idea where he got the accent.

Monday was washday at our house. Daddy filled the iron washing pot with water he had drawn from the well, a bucket at a time. He put wood around the iron pot and heated the water for mother to wash our clothes for the week. Daddy put the washtubs on the west side of the little house so mother could work in the shade, out of the hot sun. There were three tubs: a washtub, rinsing tub and bluing tub. Mother used a washing board to scrub out the stains on our work clothes.

One Monday morning, Traveling John showed up with his travel pack on his back. After a greeting, he asked for a glass of water. Mother left her work, went in the house, chipped some ice at the icebox and brought Traveling John a glass of cold ice water. He took his time drinking, and thanked her several times for her kindness. He then opened his pack and tried to make some sales. He held up a pair of ladies underwear to mother and said, "Step-ins, step-ins, these are pretty step-ins." He dangled the underwear as he talked, but mother didn't see the need. She was washing underwear for all of us. He turned to me and held up a pair of suspenders, saying, "Boy, if you wear these they will keep you from getting arthritis." I was young and frisky, could run like a bullet, so I declined his offer. Traveling John didn't make a sale with us that day, but he sure got a good cold drink of water.

I wish I had not passed up my chance to avoid today's aches and pains. Oh, my back hurts. My left shoulder tingles when I raise my arm. My fingers don't all bend fist-tight. Sometimes we miss tomorrow's blessings by passing opportunities by with a smile. Oh Traveling John, where are you? With the pack he carried on his back, now I understand why he wore suspenders.

Crow's Elbow

The doctor said he had seen the same symptoms in patients who were tennis players, fishermen, and clergy. The elbow swells and is extremely painful following vigorous activity. He had seen the same thing in a few politicians, but it was usually in both elbows. Some common names are: Tennis Elbow, Fisherman's Elbows, Crow's Elbow and Election Elbow.

As to clergy, he said Crow's Elbow usually showed up in pastors of congregations with strong traditions, emphasis on doctrinal purity and longer pastorates. Ironically, he had not seen many young pastors with Crow's Elbow. Occasionally, there is a wife or husband he sees with the same painful symptoms, usually in a home where decisions are not shared. It is not a gender disease.

Treatment is rather simple in nature, but hard to follow. The tennis player is to rest from the game, 'til nature heals. The fisherman is to lay the rod and reel aside for a while. The clergy is a little harder to treat. Think about Jesus who couldn't please everyone. Rest up from saluting flying crows, be nice to people, and close to God. The politician has a double cure: be a real person and protect social security. As to spousal domination, just say, "Do it yourself."

It is comforting to know Crow's Elbow is not just a clergy ailment. Thank God there is a treatment. And as a last resort in determination, if Bo Jackson can play professional football on a hip joint replacement, can others function competitively with elbow replacements? In modern medicine it is a new world every day. With God every day has always been new.

Honk If You Love Jesus

Possum Creek is one of my favorite places to fish. The water is quiet. Trees are beautiful. Turkeys call and geese honk. There is an island where the geese love to gather. The foxes and coyotes cannot invade their space. Sometimes a hen goose sits on a nest above one of my favorite fishing spots. I call it Bob's Cave. The geese move over the lake, often in pairs. My fishing buddy asks, "Why is that one honking?" I said, "She is asking,' why are you going that way?'."

People driving cars and trucks honk a lot. At the red light someone changes lanes and you hear a honk. A car turns in your direction and someone is smiling, waving and honking at a friend. A teenager drives out of the parking lot after school and honks three times at friends. The honk says, "Do you see me? Do you see me? I see you!" A fast driver in the right lane speeds ahead of two lanes to make a sudden change of mind to cross over to the Raceway for gas. "Honk, honk, honk" is what you hear from the whizzed-by drivers, thankful their front bumpers are still in place.

In a big city or at the country crossroads you may see a sign on the back bumper of a pickup truck that says, "Honk if you love Jesus." On a visit to San Juan, Puerto Rico, I was deeply moved by the love for Jesus. It was a different driving style---move here, let me in the lane, I got to turn, you stopped too quickly, I am tired of waiting, etc. In the states, it is---stop combing your hair, get off the cell phone, quit reading the headlines, you are driving too slowly, etc. It finally dawned on me that even our secular problems can help promote our faith. It may work out better in the long run if we just interpret the impatience as "Honk if you love Jesus.' That could stimulate patience in an often crazy world.

My friend of forty years died last night. I went to visit him this Sunday morning during church time. The man at the desk did not give me a room number. He said, "Call the family." It was an ethical way of saying my friend has ended his 89 years on this earth. Jay was an auto dealer. He loved cars and loved to sell them. We purchased three from him over the years as our family added drivers. Our three cars had horns. We could honk. Jay told me a few days ago he had purchased another car. Two now sit at his back door.

I was prayerful as I sat in the turn lane at the red light to go to Jay's house to see his family. The light changed to green and a green arrow. Before I pressed the pedal there was a honk. I turned and pulled to the right lane and let the lady pass in her red car. She was a'justin' her hat as she passed and sped through the yellow light at 10 a.m. on Sunday morning. Yes, all the signs were there. She was late and she loved Jesus. Or maybe the honk I heard was at the "Pearly Gates of Heaven." Jay stopped and honked to St. Peter, "I love Jesus, too." As I turned the next corner I heard in my mind, "Let him in. He is one of mine, too." AMEN.

Letter to Christian Church Worship Bulletin Service 1986

And 3 Messages from "Hear the Word of the Lord" series:

First Christian Church
Disciples of Christ
700 North Wood Avenue
Florence, Alabama 35630
Telephone: (256) 764-2192

September 27, 1985

Mr. Stuart Johnston
Christian Board of Publication
Beaumont and Pine Boulevard
Box 179
St. Louis, Mo 63316

Dear Mr. Johnston:

    Thank you for the opportunity to write one of the weekly messages for the Christian Church Workshop Bulletin Service, September 14, 1986. Enclosed are three messages based on Hosea 4:1-3, 5:15-6:6, from which you may choose one for your purposes. I appreciate the opportunity to contribute to this important service of CBP to the churches.

                                      Sincerely,
                                      Robert H. Stegall

RHS/lh
Enc. (3)

Hear the Word of the Lord:
    a) In Our Senior Years
    b) In Our Personal Suffering
    c) In a World of Temptations

Hear the Word of the Lord (The Senior Years)

Hosea 4:1-3, 5:15-6:6

The old man is up before daylight every day. The joggers see him pull out of his driveway at 6 a.m. He is retired. His wife was at home as long as he could care for her. Sometimes she was a little confused, but he was always there to help. He puttered around the house, peeped around his paper, stayed close to home—keeping an eye on her.

He is probably driving into the parking lot at the nursing home by now. He will say hello to his love, and give her a good morning kiss as if he had slept as near as the next bed. She will smile and be reassured. Who knows how long they have been in love. The church celebrated their 50th wedding anniversary with them some years back. Someone from the church still takes roses to her bedside table. He's the treasurer in the Men's Bible Class. Last Sunday, the class sang happy birthday to him and gave him a plaque of Hosea 6:6, "For I desire steadfast love and not sacrifice, the knowledge of God, rather than burnt offerings." As far as we know, they have been in love forever.

Hear the Word of the Lord
(In Our Personal Suffering)

Hosea 4:1-3, 5:15-6.6

Hosea realized the grief of God over Israel's idolatry through the adultery of his wife, Gomer. Personal suffering gave him a deeper insight into God's pleading love for his people.

God's charge was, "There is no faithfulness or kindness, and no knowledge of God in the land." (Hosea 4:1b) If the absence of these things takes away God's joy in his people, then the restoration of these qualities can increase the joy of the Lord.

The Church Board voted to enlarge the doors of the restrooms, making them accessible to the handicapped. A Sunday School teacher opened the class with prayer, and taught the lesson on "Doing the Word". The preacher preached from the Gospel lesson. A special day offering was taken to undergird the whole church mission.

Prayers were offered for suffering farmers and workers whose plants had closed. Greeters were announced for next month's worship services. Love reached out to broken hearts and included them. No one left the worship of God feeling as a stranger.

Hearing and doing God's word brings new life.

Hearing the Word of God In Our World of Temptations

Hosea 4:1-3, 5:15-6:6

Hosea learned from the faithlessness of his wife, Gomer, a deeper insight into God's love for a wayward people. "Let us press on to know the Lord; his going forth is as sure as the dawn; he will come to us as the showers, as the spring rains water the earth." (Hosea 6:3)

The worship of God is at the heart of faith and the renewal of hope. Christians gather today in the cities and suburbs, towns and crossroads, to "Hear the word of the Lord." Daily news rehearses the plights and dilemmas of a world that is strife-filled and misguided in idolatry. Worship means a returning to the Lord, affirming Him and being healed.

We hear the news, the traffic, a sonic boom, thunder, a conversation, and a hundred voices wooing us with promises of purchases that will make us winsome, attractive, and happy. God's word calls us to a wholeness, "Come, let us return to the Lord: for he has torn, that he may heal us; he has stricken, and he will bind us up." (Hosea 6:1) Being faithful to God begins with hearing His word and continues with doing His word.

Is A Squirrel Out There Yet?

Every morning I look out the bay window in the kitchen and ask "Is a squirrel out there yet?" As I sip a cup of coffee, I ponder the whereabouts of the squirrel. Today the metal bird feeder was swinging on the bird feeder post. I have never seen a bird swing that feeder so I know a squirrel was close by. Sure enough, there it was, back on the ground.

That squirrel is an "absolute genius." It jumps past the tin shields I put around the feeder post. It can climb out on a limb to the very end and keep its balance. It can hang upside down by its hind feet and eat out of the feeder down to the last few seeds. It can swipe out the seeds and snack before it goes to the oak tree. Friends gave me two metal bird feeders to replace the wooden feeders. The squirrel mastered the challenge. I am thinking about covering the tin shield with olive oil, but it will probably make a slide out of my work.

Hatchie River Bottom was the place I learned to appreciate squirrels. It was my reward to go squirrel hunting after preparing two sermons and Wednesday Bible Study each week. The peace and quiet was a gift of God, in addition to learning from the squirrels. They hid behind limbs. They carried nuts in their jaws back to the nest. They buried food in the ground, which meant they planted trees. They jumped from tree limb to tree limb better than Tarzan.

Frank, my friend, brought me a squirrel tail one day. He said, "I know you make fishing lures. Maybe you can make a hair jig out of this squirrel tail." Hair jigs are good bait. The squirrel reminds me of a squirrel tail a high school friend tied to the radio antenna on his truck. Most anybody can find a squirrel tail. I could have picked up one today. It was in the middle of the road. One thing the squirrel has never mastered is crossing the road to the other side. That is why I ask myself every morning, "Is a squirrel out there yet?" See you on the other side.

A Tale of Leaf Burning

We took our grandchild to Sunday dinner at a favorite restaurant. Justin was excited and curious. While we placed our order, he looked around and asked, "Why is that next room smoky?" It was an opportunity to pass on the tale of the leaf burning tradition.

Justin, thousands of years ago our ancestors lived in caves. In the fall of the year they gathered mounds of dried leaves, foretelling the end of a season, and piled them in the rear of the winter caves. The leaves reminded them of the gathered fruits of the trees: hickory nuts, persimmons, walnuts, pecans, apples, peaches, plums, the bounty of fresh and dried fruits for a winter's feast. The store of crisp dried leaves was fertile tender for warm cave fires when cold winds blew, deep snows fell, and life was held in the cold grip of winter.

Over the centuries leaf burning became a ritual of clan gathering and brew sipping. Creative clans added spices and aromatics to their leaves, and became adept at identifying fellow leaf burners by the odor of their hair or clothing. As time passed, our ancestors moved out of caves into dwellings. In the fall of the year, they kept alive the ancient leaf burning ritual by raking leaves in their yards and setting them afire to smolder and burn for days. Enthusiastic participation concerned the city fathers because a smoky haze engulfed their community. An ordinance was passed prohibiting mass leaf burning.

Today, the ancient leaf burning ritual is kept alive by a faithful few. Leaf burning rooms have been reserved in restaurants, public buildings, and sacred places. It lives on in the swirls and curls of commuters. Lone figures take their places away from the crowd to offer up the ritual of remembrance of days long gone in warm caves stocked with fruits of autumn trees.

Justin, the leaf burning rooms are a monument to a way of the life fast passing. They are reminders of our ancestors and how they survived in caves. One day there may be no leaf burning rooms. There will be no remembrance of an ancient tradition, only a tale about leaf burning that grandfathers tell their grandchildren at Sunday dinners.

A Better Perspective

From the day we arrived, we talked about remodeling the kitchen. When one moves, it is more apparent that appliances may not match, and an older house has the scars of previous use. We started our fish fries immediately, even if the kitchen was out of joint. Time has proven if one waits till everything matches before inviting guests, invitations may go unnoticed and love unshared. On the other hand, there is a false wisdom that says save the remodeling till the inviting is over lest the traffic mar your handiwork. But who wants to be a professional guest?

At the beginning of the fifth year in our house, we did start remodeling the kitchen. We added new appliances, counter tops, blinds, wallpaper, etc., and it was all color coordinated. Perhaps our guests would like it, and every day it was our joy. You know how it is with human nature. It doesn't seem like yours until you've put your hand to it. Guess that is why some folks at church still say "them" and "ya'll", while others say "ours". We all know it really is "His".

How we got rid of the replaced things is another matter. Some we gave away. Some we threw in the trash. Some we sold. It took three months to realize that we didn't need a dishwasher sitting unconnected in the garage. It was becoming a tombstone. Finally, we advertised in the want ads. After consultation with a salesperson, it read: "For sale: Green used dishwasher. $30.00." The first caller bought it. Going the second mile, I guaranteed it would work or money back. The man called the next day and reported a leak. I sent him the $30.00 and asked for no return. I still wonder if it developed a leak, or if I was taken.

Sometimes we need perspective worse than anything else. It could have been a throw-away instead of $30.00. And $30.00 didn't make a dent in the cost of a new kitchen. I guess the clincher was when I found $30.00 on the steps going in to the Garth Brooks Concert. There must be a million ways to keep from enjoying a new kitchen. What a shame.

A Mixed Bag

Baseball means very little to me until the World Series. I usually begin watching the last four teams in the playoffs, and then the last two for the World Series. In the series, there is the mounting tension of competition, and finally, the Agony and the Ecstasy. One team cries with joy and the other cries with defeat, salty tears that reflect a mixed bag of joy and sorrow.

The artist knows the beauty of the painting is in the balance of light and shadow. The light is too bright for beauty without the shadow, and the shadow is too dull without the light. Spiritually, we know with the psalmist that the contrasts of moods and events give the opposite its meaning and content. Constancy may father contentment, but variety can lift the spirit. The psalmist speaks of the swing of the pendulum in optimistic terms:

> "For his anger is but for a moment, and his favor is for a lifetime. Weeping may tarry for the night, but joy comes in the morning. (Psalm 30:5)

The camera captures and frames the final moments of the two best teams of the leagues... the last pitch, the last out, and the game is over. One team leaps on the field with joy. They scramble to touch each other and personify the team spirit of cooperation. The other team sits stunned in the shadow of the dugout until the light of reality dawns when someone says, "Wait until next year."

Life is lived somewhere between the wedding and funeral. There is singing and dancing at one house, and across the street a black ribbon hangs quietly, flapping effortlessly in a chilly wind. The singing won't last forever with the wedding party, and the black ribbon will take turns with the houses on the block. No one gets all the light, and no one gets all the shadow. It is a mixed bag. Thank God for those who specialize in putting rejoicing in context, or grief in a larger frame by saying, "Wait till next time."

In time, we all will have sufficient opportunity for both. Let us rejoice in our God who holds our times and the hope of next time in His hands.

Chapter 7
Put The Plow In The Ground

Put the Plow in the Ground

Sometimes when I visit the family on the farm in Tennessee, I drive the tractor. Tractors cost thousands of dollars and pull plows that cost thousands of dollars. Driven by diesel engines, the driver has at his command great teams of horsepower. A common mistake of the infrequent driver is failing to release the plow after turning around at the end of the field. Nothing ever gets plowed unless one puts the plow in the ground.

As we begin this new year, no aim or goal can be accomplished unless we put the plow in the ground. Since we are creatures of habit, it is important to begin spiritually healthy habits in January. Getting anywhere always begins with beginning. So, put the plow in the ground at the beginning of the year. It is the little streams that finally make up the big rivers that flow into the ocean. Jesus said, "He who is faithful in very little is faithful also in much." (Luke 16:10) Release the plow into the fertile and unbroken soil of your new year, another promising gift of God to us.

A Father Responds

One of the nice things about being a father is enjoying your grown children. You reap the dividends of the years of building good memories—fishing, camping, snowmen, blast-offs in new shoes, eating watermelon, befriending the neighborhood dog, Sunday dinners, going to the farm, peanuts in a coke, riding in the back of the truck, searching for lunch money, church, etc.

I am enjoying being a middle-aged father. Now, I can discuss things that are important to me with the children. They buy me clothes, gadgets, tools, and fishing equipment. They call and check on me. They are concerned about my health and happiness. They invite me to their homes. It is a comfort to know that in all of life's changes I can count on them.

Today, I am indebted to our children. I tried harder because they depended on me. I learned how to endure unpleasantness to keep life stable for them. I have been more careful of my words and deeds lest I embarrass our children or they become ashamed of me. The respect of our children has been a priority. I am a student now. They teach me new ideas and challenge me with new gadgets. They try to keep the rut from overpowering me.

Things are as they should be. I am learning to turn loose. They are learning to hold on. A father eventually works himself out of a job. He thinks, "I must help them to learn to get along without me. I won't always be here." When Dad hears a child pray, "Our Father, who art in heaven..." he hears the sound of success. Taking a child's hand and placing it in the hands of "Our Heavenly Father" is the crowning success of being a parent. Happy Father's Day!

Cultivating a Thankful Spirit

A thankful spirit is not automatic. Thanksgiving is the fruit of "Count Your Many Blessings, Name Them One by One." There is no better way to grow a thankful attitude than to make a list.

- Pictures of my family and their unfailing love
- The gift of "Ducks in Flight", the handwork of a wife from high school sweetheart days
- A basket of apples and a vase of flowers from friends
- A college annual, full of friends and precious memories
- A church directory and the precious privilege of awakening each day to shepherd God's flock
- Visitor's cards on my desk from Sunday worship
- A flip chart from the meeting of a Sunday School Class in our home, seeking guidance in reaching out
- Bibles, old and new, underlined, ragged—gifts from those who believed in the Word and me
- Outdated correspondence from a Billy Graham Crusade, with fruits yet being harvested
- A Year Book of the Christian Church, holding treasures of loving friends and congregations
- Books that challenge my heart and mind, and pull me close to God and a loving Christ
- A wastebasket, that I can use every day to trash instead of stash
- A phone call of one wanting to register for Wednesday morning Bible Study
- A map to a home party of our newest Sunday School Class
- An "Estimate of Giving Card" to record thanks-living hopes
- A quiet moment in which to "Count God's Blessings and be thankful"
- America, Freedom, Opportunity, Veterans

Sometimes the spirit of thanksgiving may hide. Scratch around. Look. Listen. Reflect. Oh, there you are! Happy Thanksgiving!

What Every Father Should Know

II Samuel 14:28-15:6   Ephesians 6:1-4

Fathers, do not provoke your children to anger, but bring them up in the discipline and instruction of the Lord. (Ephesians 6:4)

My Mean Father

I had the meanest father in the world. Other kids could talk back to their mothers, disobey them in front of company, and tell their mothers what they were not going to do. Dad demanded I respect mother 24 hours a day, 7 days a week, 365 days a year. I still have the hang-over of saying "Yes, Ma'am" and "No, Sir" to my parents.

Other kids could run out of the house and slam the door, but I had to go back and "close it right" and keep closing it until it finally met my father's approval. He marked me for life with a dislike for slammed doors, and I often daydream of what I missed.

Many of my friends had nothing to do in the summer but rest and relax. My father made me work with him and the rest of the family. I spent long days working by his side, laughing, talking, and teasing. Some of my lucky friends had all the time to themselves, and were not bothered by their fathers.

I sometimes imagine what I might be today if my father had not harassed me with his demands that I respect mother, the property of others, and the responsibility of doing my share of the work. What is even worse? I, too, became a mean father. Thank God!

The Home Coming

Last week I was invited by the Humboldt, Tennessee Ministerial Alliance to return to our hometown, and speak at the Prayer Breakfast during the Strawberry Festival. The sign at the city limits read, "Humboldt, Home of the Strawberry Festival, Our Home and Your Home". Although not a full-time resident since 1953, the year I left for college, it will always be our hometown. I was glad to go back and say "thank you" to family, church, school, community, and friends. A good hometown will always be a great asset in life, whether a resident or visitor.

One of the milestones of life is learning to say 'forty". Often there is public notice of birthday parties with banners and ads that read, "Lordy, Lordy, Bob is 40." At forty, one can be happily intentional. It was forty years ago that I left Humboldt, to study for the ministry. In June, I will return to celebrate our fortieth class reunion.

Going home is relative---going home to Tennessee, Alabama, or Arkansas. If home is where the heart is, then my cup overflows. I'm thankful I can say "forty".

The Hope of Christmas

The older I get, the more I remember Christmas past. I remember fireworks, a windup Caterpillar tractor, Red Ryder gloves, family and friends, and that Christmas Eve was the longest day of the year. I could spend the rest of my life just thinking about Christmas past.

Isaiah holds up a poetic picture of Christmas future:

> Behold, I am doing a new thing; now it springs forth, do you not perceive it? I will make a way in the wilderness and rivers in the desert. The wild beasts will honor me, the jackals and the ostriches; For I give water in the wilderness, and rivers in the desert, to give drink to my chosen people, the people I have formed for myself that they might declare my praise.
>
> Isaiah 43:19-21

Christmas is not just what God has done, but what God will do—the Impossible; peace among superpowers, organ transplants, singing in the cemetery, sharing by those who have little, caring by those who have plenty, forgiveness, new beginnings, freedom from the chains of habit, electronic journeys, power to move mountains, bridges to cross valleys, brotherhood and sisterhood, a love that is strong enough to hold on and wise enough to turn loose.

Pray, let us rejoice in our God's Christmas gift, who slows our rapid pace of living down for a day while we look at a baby in a manger with the promise: "BEHOLD, I AM DOING A NEW THING!" If God has His way, we have not seen anything yet!

A Tear and a Smile

Two things are more eloquent than ten thousand words—a tear and a smile. Both are communication at the deepest level.

One of the most touching pictures is a lone Indian sitting on his horse overlooking a valley of human litter, with a single tear upon his cheek.

The chill in a room for a stranger is warmed by a single smile carefully aimed at anxious eyes.

Tears and smiles are identical twins of the mother of feelings and the father of caring. One wears a "Have a Happy Day" face with turned up lips and other wears a frowning "Misery Loves Company" face. Tears and smiles are both fleet footed---as quick as lightning, high energy levels of communication.

Last week I waited at the intersection while children crossed the busy street on their way to school. Four children started across. Three finished and turned to encourage the last. A little girl, six or seven, made a game out of limping on leg braces bound to tiny shoes. Her pigtails danced as she joyfully crossed a sea of asphalt, smiling and laughing as she went.

For a moment, I was a lone Indian overlooking a valley filled with courage and beauty---and there was a tear on my cheek. The sight of great courage does me that way. But, for the life of me, I cannot understand why I had the tear and she had the smile. Ah, sweet mystery!

Paul says a Christian has a double portion through caring, "Rejoice with those who rejoice, weep with those who weep." (Romans 12:15) No wonder we say, "I laughed until I cried." Thank God, we can also say, "I cried until I laughed."

As you know, twins love to trade places.

A Salute to Willie Frank

Willie Frank lived on a red hill pasture covered with sage grass on the south side of Sugar Creek. On the railroad side of that hill, his father had the finest watermelon patch in the country. It was cursed with a line of trees between it and the house, keeping Mr. Sumner from watching the growing melons. One giant melon must have weighed a hundred pounds. Someone had shaded it with a brush arbor while it ripened, and both crows and boys respected it as first fruits, holy unto the Lord.

In his early twenties, Willie Frank was eager to get away from the tin roofed four-room house of home. He went to work for Papa on the farm. It was only a mile from his home, but Willie Frank was on his way in the world.

Willie was jittery and skittish. When he talked, he cocked his head to one side as if propping up on some invisible force that gave him both authority and courage to speak.

He slept upstairs at Papa's and often spoke of experiences with strange visitors at night. More than once he reported waking to find an old man with a long beard bending over him and breathing in his face. The nightly visitor was so troublesome that one morning he asked Granny if someone had died in the room upstairs.

A letter came from Franklin D. Roosevelt, President of the United States, requesting he report for duty to serve his country. The skittish Tennessee boy did not want to go—but he went. His mother placed a miniature flag in her front window, and his father talked war over the waters with new interest. One day, the local paper carried the news—WILLIE FRANK SUMNER KILLED IN ACTION.

Today there is a sea of wheat waving tall proud heads of grain on the old red hill pasture. Yesterday, there was a 100 lb. watermelon, taking its time getting ripe. But the finest thing that old red hill will ever produce is WILLIE FRANK SUMNER.

Jesus said, "Greater love has no man than this, that he lay down his life for his friends." (John 15:13)

Courage is not freedom from fear, but doing the honorable thing, even when afraid. On Memorial Day, we salute the Willie Frank Sumners. Their bravery still speaks.

Farewell and Hello

We have been challenged to make many changes in our lives and loyalties this year. Kay and I said farewell to our house of 18 Christmases. We left Sunday dinners with our children. We told a dear flock I was now a lifetime friend but no longer their minister. We gave away books, had a garage sale, hauled loads of stuff to the city dump. We said goodbye to some favorite fishing holes.

In January, we moved to First Christian in Little Rock. We have been busy learning names, streets, phone numbers, addresses, traditions, and history. We have a new house, a new car, a new challenge, new friends, and soon a new grandbaby. We have a new set of obligations and responsibilities, challenges and opportunities, and fishing holes.

In 1987, we said "farewell" and "hello". It is a good year, for in the Lord it is a year of precious blending of the past and present. We count our blessings and give thanks to the Lord. As pilgrims, we rest in the Lord and rejoice in His goodness, even as the Psalmist says, "Thou crownest the year with thy bounty; the tracks of thy chariot drip with fatness". (Psalm 65:11) Happy Thanksgiving to you. May the Lord bless you in the blending of your precious past, challenging present, and hopeful future.

Families Recovering Happy Holidays!

It may be said of holidays, "These are the best of times, and the worst of times." Anticipations are so high, and seldom can reality match the dream. While children see visions of sugarplums, adults are prone to just see pumpkins. The older we are, the larger the pumpkins. It is most gratifying when pumpkin-expecting adults see sugarplums again with children.

A grand patriarch Clark Stegall, my father, died mid March, 1984. It was a long illness. He died at home in his own bed in a house he built, and on land he tilled and loved. One morning in early March, there was a thin crust of snow over the yard that prompted thoughts of Shakespeare's line in Julius Caesar, "Beware the Ides of March"—a hint of things to come in the words of the soothsayer. And it came just like the Bible said it would, "It is appointed unto man once to die." (Hebrews 9:27)

Grief is a personal experience. It makes no difference how many times one has served as a pallbearer, how many funerals one has attended, or how many pets one has buried. Grief must be personalized with cards, notes, markers, food, prayers, flowers, candles, memorials, tears, etc. Often, grief is punctuated with anger and criticisms or flights of freedom and busyness. Is some culture, people wear a black arm band or veil to say publicly, "I am in grief and may not be myself. Take care how you approach me." But life hastens on, and few can afford that privilege.

Thanks be to God, who lifts the fog of grief, and lets the sunshine of His love dry tears and put smiles on sad faces. Blessed be the God of Isaiah and Handel's Messiah, who said, "Comfort, comfort my people, says your God. Speak tenderly to Jerusalem, and cry to her, that her warfare is ended, that her iniquity is pardoned... prepare the way of the Lord, and make straight in the desert a highway for our God." We may wander in circles, but the shortest distance through grief is a straight teary line, under the wing of the Almighty.

Another Holiday came at the home place. The kitchen was filled with aromas of baked chicken and dressing, fried ham, turnips, greens, baked sweet potatoes topped with marshmallows, rolls, and strawberry cake. There was laughter, joke telling, and reminiscing. Four generations filled three rooms. A two-year old played with pan lids in the kitchen. There was chatter in the den. New patriarchs snoozed in the living room.

Thank God for families recovering, for homes that can withstand extremes, and for the visions of sugarplums. By the grace of God, endings are places of new beginnings. "Therefore, I remind you to rekindle the gift of God that is within you...for God did not give us a spirit of timidity, but a spirit of power and love and self-control." (II Timothy 1:6-7) Merry Christmas!

Chapter 8
Bottom Line Living

Bottom Line Living

There are variables we cannot control in our lives and experiences. It is important what the bottom line is for each of us. The best bottom line I can think of is love, and love means many things to people. Sometimes love is gentle. Sometimes love is tough. At times, we hold on tight because we love. At other times, we turn loose because we love.

Deuteronomy 6:4 introduces the motivation that is capable of calling the best of God's people:
"Hear, O Israel: The Lord our God is one Lord, and you shall love the Lord your God with all your heart, and with all your soul, and with all your might." (Deuteronomy 6: 4-5)

Paul writes the Corinthians, and addresses "the more excellent way" of seasoned love:
"When I was a child, I spoke like a child, I thought like a child, I reasoned like a child; but when I became a man, I gave up childish ways. For now we see in a mirror dimly, but then face to face... So faith, hope, love, abide these three: but the greatest of these is love." (I Corinthians 13:11-12,13)

Our personal goals and ambitions may be hammered out on the anvil of love. Sometimes we know what we want to be. At other times, we may be shaped by what we do not want to be. Loving may mean stretching our limits for someone else. It is hard to live seasoned love without drawing some lines. Good love should have good boundaries. Happy Valentine's Day!!

Homecoming is Like...

Sunday was a great homecoming for us as Brother Dan and Margaret Kenner shared with us in worship and fellowship. We had a great attendance with good opportunity for visiting with members and friends. Thanks to all who contributed to the beautiful spirit of the day. The joy of a homecoming always brings to mind Psalm 133:

> Behold, how good and pleasant it is
> when brothers dwell in unity!
>
> It is like the precious oil upon the
> head, running down on the collar of his robes!
>
> It is like the dew of Hermon, which
> falls on the Mountains of Zion!
>
> For there the Lord has commanded the
> blessing: life for evermore.

Our images of homecoming joy may be expressed in more relevant terminology:

> Behold, how good and pleasant it is
> when brothers and sisters dwell peacefully.
>
> It is like a glass of cold iced tea,
> with a squeeze of lemon on a hot summer day.
>
> It is like hearing an old friend call
> your name from across a crowded room.
>
> It is like a bouquet of flowers plucked

from the fields of yesterday, that drop sweet petals down a worn path of memories.

It is like a family sitting by a warm hearth on a winter's evening, listening to stories, eating popcorn, laughing, and watching children smile.

Homecoming is a feast of remembering--- a blessing God gives, and repeats a million times in memory.

Happy Thanksgiving

Who do we thank? We can thank parents for love, friends for faithfulness, families for steadfastness, and thousands of people for thousands of favors. One of the graces of life is the ability to express appreciation for the contributions of others to our welfare. Sometimes pride, self-centeredness, or forgetfulness robs us of the double pleasure of saying, "thank you." Somehow we get tempted to think of what we deserve from others, rather than our indebtedness to others for what we cannot buy. When you step safely from a plane, after being 35,000 feet in the sky, a "thank you" can remind us how indebted we are to others every day.

Who do we thank for a beautiful November sunset? Who do we thank for a flight of ducks? Who do we thank for a grandchild? Who gets the thanks for a "give and take" kind of love that soars through a 50th Wedding Anniversary? Who do you thank for a church that keeps reaching its arms towards the whole world? Who do you thank for triumph in illness, perseverance in disappointment, and forgiveness in the presence of transgression?

I am a firm believer in families worshipping together. Wiggly children need to see moms and dads, grandmas and grandpas, brothers and sisters bowing their heads in worship. It is important for children to try to understand why adults manage to sit still and quietly, bowing their heads in reverence to Almighty God, "maker of heaven and earth." It is important for children to see others offering gifts, and singing hymns of praise in thanksgiving to God.

"Thank you" is the stuff from which a triumphant spirit is made. Sometimes we thank people. Sometimes we thank God. Sometimes we thank both. "Bless the Lord, O my soul, and forget not all His benefits." (Psalms 103:2) Happy Thanksgiving.

Ten Guides for Church Growth

Everyday I work some in my garden. It is the best garden I can remember. One principle I have continually honored in this dry year is "water frequently". The Lord has honored those garden principles with green beans, potatoes, onions, squash, tomatoes, okra, and sweet corn.

In the last few years, there has been a wide study of Church Growth Principles. Why do some churches grow? Why do some churches decline? One of my goals is to learn and apply Church Growth Principles in God's Garden.

Here are a few of those principles you and I can honor:

1. <u>Nothing</u> is a complete success unless it involves someone new.
2. The nursery is the second most important place in Church life. The sanctuary is first.
3. Music needs to be in variety and triumphant. Not everyone has the same tastes.
4. Property concerns should not dominate program concerns. Programs attract and minister to people.
5. New members need to be incorporated within a group within one year or they may remain aloof or disappear.
6. The staff exists to serve Christ and the Church. Longer ministries tend to be more productive.
7. The most important activities are Lord's Day. Other events are secondary.
8. Biblical preaching and emphasis on worshiping God are primary needs to be met.
9. People tend to avoid churches in conflict.
10. Realistic numerical goals are a way of focusing and evaluating Church Growth Emphasis.

When these Ten Commandments of Church Growth are honored, we will see God's Garden flourish. Thanks to our Church Growth Panel for helping us identify these Church Growth Principles. I invite you to post them on the refrigerator door or a mirror to memorize and apply daily in your walk with the Lord in His Church.

A Two Bus Church

I believe the time has come for us to commit ourselves to being a two-bus church. We have two priority commitments: ministering to youth and reaching young families, and ministering with our Senior Adult members.

Our youth need the church van for Terrific Tuesdays, Scout weekend trips, Sunday evening youth programs, camps, conferences, annual Philmont Scout trip to New Mexico, annual Smoky Mountain trip, Memphis, Dallas, etc.

We need a bus for our Senior Adults to enlarge our Sunday bus ministry, provide transportation to all church activities for our older members, and to organize monthly trips such as: circus, River Cruise, Passion Play in Eureka Springs, heritage tours to Cane Ridge, Nashville, St. Louis, etc. I believe our Senior Adults deserve a bus that has comfortable seats, handrails, low steps, walk-in aisles, etc.

Our Long Range Planning Committee proposed we replace the church van in 1995. I believe we need to speed up that proposal to adding a Church bus for Senior Adults as soon as possible.

Becoming a "Two-Bus Church" will be an expression of our commitment to minister to <u>all</u> our members to the best of our ability. I have discussed this with our elders and asked for their support. One of our regular Sunday van riders committed $100.00 toward purchasing a bus. I think the time has come. I believe the money will come.

A New Beginning

And Jesus said, "Father, forgive them for they know not what they do." And they cast lots to divide his garments. (Luke 23:34)

Last fall, my old lawnmower of 11 years finally gave up the ghost. No amount of coaxing, caressing, or condemning has stirred a spark of life in it. It was a faithful soldier and an avid worker. In tribute, I am almost inclined to paint it before I let the junkman have it. It really was never the same after I hit a stump. But somehow the more attention it required, the more attached I became. Yet, for all my attachment—it has no regard for the grass anymore.

Perhaps it still has some fitting use. If there is a coon dog cemetery, then why not a lawnmower cemetery? But it would have to be kept meticulously clean or the tribute would be voided by weeds. Perhaps it could be mounted on a marble slab in one of our beautiful parks, and the trade name removed to be anonymously inscribed "To the Unknown Lawnmower." Perhaps, then, the world would no longer take short grass, edged curbs and manicured lawns for granted.

It seems so hard to begin anew when we are so attached to the old. While saving calendars may be a good hobby, there is something in us that demands— "but what about today?" The death of Jesus puts to rest the past failures to do God's will. At the cross, Jesus fulfills the legal demands of the law, and calls attention to the grace of God—His love and mercy—in which we are given a new beginning. Calvary is the greatest measure of God's love for us. All our excuses die at Golgotha, and they are replaced with reasons... "The times of ignorance God overlooked, but now he commands all men everywhere to repent." (Acts 17:30) Where can we not begin again?

Remote Cabin Fever

It was Sunday, the third day of being iced-in, and the preacher had his blue jeans on. Wonder what's on the tube? Where is the remote control?

Kenneth Copeland... standing, sitting, walking... Any notes would need wings to keep up with him. Jimmy Swaggert... riding on a white cloud of music, raising the dead from emotional rigor mortis. Jerry Falwell... flag in one hand and Bible in the other, calling the weak to strength and the wayward to repentance. Robert Schuler... melting hardened hearts with the sunshine of his smile and thoughts of new possibilities. Jim Bakker... building Heritage Village, a spiritual refuge for the world-weary, the inspiration of color, music, and testimony patterned after "the best of Carson."

The variety of religious offerings were as rich as the cafeteria of a world's fair. Whatever suits your fancy... Italian, Chinese, Mexican, Cajun, American, Soul. Uh oh! 12 o'clock! Is the bean soup ready? Time to mute the remote. Two things about TV church... I can get out on time, and I miss my church family. Hope to see you Sunday.

Faith vs. Frustration

One of our deepest needs is to feel that we are in control of our lives. Consequently, one of our worst fears is that we will lose control of deciding our destiny.

The sleet and ice of this past weekend makes havoc of our calendars, dates, and appointments. There are so many things we feel we have to do, but don't---need to do, but can't. So we cancelled worship, Sunday School, Beliefs and Practices, Youth, PIE, Elders, Scouts, Bethel, choir, etc. Priorities shifted from options to survival.

Perhaps our commitments are at times not only expressions of our goals, but also of our pride and arrogance. James writes, Come now, you who say, "Today or tomorrow we will go into such and such a town and spend a year there, and trade, and get gain;" whereas you do not know about tomorrow…Instead you ought to say "If the Lord wills, we shall live and we shall do this or that." As it is, you boast in your arrogance. (James 4:13-16)

Certainly, we need to plan, schedule, and make meaningful commitments for the future. If there is any lesson in a blanket of six inches of ice it is: Who knows what tomorrow will bring? Trust in the Lord each day and seek His will in paralyzing ice or liberating sunshine. Faith is a matter of heart, not weather.

Hey Coach, Got a Minute?

    Chances are I will never have the privilege of meeting former head football coach of the Dallas cowboys, Tom Landry, but I plan to see and hear him Saturday morning, June 3, 9:30-11:30 at Barton Coliseum. I will be at the church parking lot at 8:30 a.m. to catch a ride on the church bus. If I get close enough to holler, I know what my first words will be: "Hey Coach, Got a Minute?", because I have some questions. My questions are about life, not football. Here is my list:

1. Coach, as one of professional football's most successful coaches, why did you ever stay associated with the Billy Graham Crusades? You could have been teaching some winning plays with that time, and some TV evangelists seem risky.
2. Coach, how do you motivate a herd of aggressive and expressive people to put their best into every effort so the whole team can achieve victory. It's so much easier to lose when each have the last word.
3. Coach, why could we not get a crowd at church on NFL Sunday when the Cowboys were in the Super Bowl, and now we can't get our crowd to Barton Coliseum on a Saturday to hear the famous Cowboy's coach, a Christian in the United Methodist Church, talk about "Life's Priorities"?
4. Coach, how do you react after giving your time 20 years with the Billy Graham Crusades and 30 years as coach of the Dallas Cowboys when you heard that familiar voice, "Hey Coach, Got a Minute"?

Coach Landry, I believe you are qualified to speak on your subject as Christian Witness about "Life's Priorities". What is God's word for us today? Thanks for taking a minute with us in Arkansas. See you at the next Billy Graham Evangelistic Crusade. Glad you like my boots and hat.

Getting on 1st Base

What is the most important aspect of a Church in the eyes of visitors? In the Minister's Class on Beliefs and Practices of the Christian Church, those present gave the following list of things about First Christian Church that attracted them.

1. Open-Minded
2. Unconditional Love
3. Acceptance
4. Friendship
5. Fellowship
6. Concern for Individuals
7. Non-Judgmental
8. Family Warmth
9. A Teaching Church
10. A Growing Church

The first thing that anyone confronts in visiting a church is attitude. If the primary need of visitors is to find a good attitude then that is the first need we want to meet. Attitude is something we all contribute. Once the primary need is met, we have the privilege of meeting secondary needs. We thank God for His love that makes a church a loving and caring community.

GOD BLESSES A CHURCH WHEN THE PEOPLE OFFER A GOOD ATTITUDE TO THE LORD.

Roads and Friends, Old and New

This Memorial Day, I reflect on the blessings of being a Christian, serving Christ on parallel roads of faith. Sunday, we honored the men and women who served in the Armed Forces during World War II from First Christian Church. In our history is written:

"Speakers from the military personnel at Camp Robinson were frequently invited to speak. On February 9, 1942, Major Yandell S. Beans, Chaplain of the 35th Division, occupied the pulpit, accompanied by a splendid band."

First Christian greeted the many young soldiers at Camp Robinson with warmth and hospitality.

In October, 1968, at Kansas City, Mo., the son of Colonel Yandell S. Beans approached me at the General Assembly to inquire of my interest in considering a call to a pastorate at Florence, Alabama, where Dr. Stanley S. Beans was an elder and interim minister, and later Dean of Education at the University of North Alabama.

After retiring from the military, Colonel Beans served as pastor of Antioch Christian Church, at Benton, Arkansas. After retiring at Antioch, he moved to Florence, Alabama, to be near his son, Dr. Stanley Beans. Colonel Beans attended First Christian at Florence, and I was his pastor until his death. His body was returned to Arkansas for burial in the National Cemetery at Little Rock.

Today, I thank God for the Christian Road---the many friends: past, present, and future; the joyous ways our lives touch; and the hope of our Eternal Home.

Unsearchable Riches of Christ
Isaiah 60:1-6   Ephesians 3:1-12

Text: To me, though I am the very least of all the saints, this grace was given, to preach to the Gentiles the unsearchable riches of Christ. (Ephesians 3:8)

Happy New Year!

Today is the last day of the year, and tomorrow we will be using a new calendar. Goodbye, 1984. Thanks for the memories. You blessed us with 52 Lord's Days, 365 sunrises and sunsets, but time is running out and now we are using the last day of the last month. Soon you will be no more... exhausted... expired... used up, filed away in the corridors of time with all that is marked PAST. Rest in peace, for with you we entomb all our frustrations, failures, sins, short-comings, and regrets.

Hello, 1985! It is good seeing you looking so well. You smell as fresh as spring flowers. You walk on tip toe. Your touch is tender, and the face of your calendar is full of innocence. You beckon us into the future. You wave to us from the mountains, and call to us from across the rivers. You are one of the messengers of God, encouraging us to break camp from a spring soon to go dry, champion our cause with a shepherd son, "The Lord is my shepherd, I shall not want..." Wait up! We are going with you. See you Sunday.

A Good Pattern for Living

Every child should have the joy of watching a mother make a dress from a pattern. I think a child learns about life by watching someone sew a dress, coat, shirt, quilt, etc. It is the lessons of the pieces, pattern, thread, stitches, and the results. Some seams must be taken out because they may not be just right—and redone more carefully.

I believe Jesus Christ is God's pattern for a beautiful world. He shows us how to love in the midst of pain, how to get angry at patterns before people, how to weep at the tomb of Lazarus, how to build other's self-esteem, how to forgive transgressions. Jesus must have watched Joseph follow many patterns in the carpenter's shop, with a hole at the exact spot or a cut at the right place.

Easter is God's reminder that He sent the perfect pattern of His Son. Jesus lived, taught the truths of God, organized Disciples, and died for having presented a perfect pattern of goodness that contradicted old patterns of tradition.

The resurrection of Christ is God's declaration that one cannot destroy God's pattern for living. No crime in the name of state or religion can do away with Christ---the living pattern, as an angel declared, "He is not here...He is risen from the dead, and He goes before you to Galilee; there you shall see Him. (Matthew 28:7). The perfect pattern lives. In Him, I find a new piece of life every day, and fresh hope for a better world.

The Quest for Character

In 1990, our Wednesday Bible Study will focus on character: "Meet 61 of God's Greatest Bible Characters." Each week, we will study the strengths and weaknesses, the flaws and the fortitude, and the multitude of values that make up the human family. We will study how God works with people, through people, around people, and in spite of people.

In 1989, we studied God's progressive revelation through <u>EVENTS</u>, from Genesis to Revelation, and I preached on each of the Books of the Bible concurrently with our study. In 1990, I will preach on the 61 <u>CHARACTERS</u> in our study. The Wednesday Study and the Sunday sermons can be a means of reflection, meditation, and molding our lives to God's intentions "made in the image of God" and "until we achieve the full measure of the stature of Christ".

During January and February, I will be preaching sermons about:

        January 7   Adam
        January 14   Eve
        January 21   Cain, Abel, Seth
        January 28   Noah and His Sons
        February 4   Abraham
        February 11   Melchizedek
        February 18   Isaac
        February 25   Jacob

In these sermons on Bible Personalities, I will be talking about the Seven Deadly Sins that break relations with God, family, and community. These seven sins are Life threatening: in the Bible, the Middle Ages, and in 1990. They are the sins of

> Apathy—I don't care
> Gluttony—I am out of control
> Anger—I will get even
> Lust—Gratification at another's expense
> Greed—Controlled by what you don't need
> Jealousy—Wishing Evil instead of Good
> Pride—A commitment to Last Year

I look forward to studying and preaching in January and February as we begin this important life-changing quest for character that multiplies the goodness and glory of God.

The Good Ole Summertime

We need to change our way of thinking about summertime. In the church, we have grown into a pattern of thinking that little happens during the summertime. We may not be allowing it to happen.

What farmer sows seed in the spring and comes back in the fall, expecting a big harvest? Who cultivates, fertilizes, waters, pulls weeds during July and August? The scriptures say repeatedly, that God has established the seasons: "Thou hast made the moon to mark the seasons; the sun knows its time for setting". (Psalm 104:19) If summertime was not important, God would have only three seasons: fall, winter, and spring.

In the seasons of church life, summertime brings three great opportunities:

1. Some families move away to new ventures, and we can give a loving farewell.
2. More people are first time worshipers during summer than any other season, because of transfers and school.
3. Vacations bring opportunities for renewal, nurturing the spirit, meeting visitors and families.

During July and August, I try to keep my time away at a minimum, lest I miss the great opportunities of summertime. Thank God, for summertime at First Christian Church. A good summer makes a fall harvest more promising. Let us put down summertime roots that God may bless us with growth; as the Psalmist says in 1:3:
> "He is like a tree, planted by streams of water,
> That yields its fruit in its season,
> And its leaf does not wither."

The Golden Growth Rule

The Golden Rule of personal conduct and good relations is: "Do unto others as you would have them do unto you". To live by that rule in all actions and reactions is to live by the proven wisdom of building and maintaining good relations. Once the rule is disregarded, gravity rules and the dominant call of downstream is heard, even in the far away mountains.

There is a Golden Rule for Churches that plan for Church Growth, which is "No group is a complete success unless it involves someone new". It really does not matter how good the punch or how abundant the cake, or how fine the singing, lessons, or fellowship---

when there is no one new, the Golden Rule for Church Growth has not been honored. What would happen in the Church if every class, fellowship, or study group appointed a "Golden Rule Chairperson" who has worked toward having someone new at every meeting. I invite you to think and pray about this Golden Rule:

> "NO GROUP IS A COMPLETE SUCCESS IN THE CHURCH, UNLESS IT INVOLVES SOMEONE NEW."

I do not think success can be measured in terms of how many members were present, but who was there that is new. It is reported of the dynamic church of Acts 2:47, "...Praising God and having favor with all the people. And the Lord added to their number, day by day, those who were being saved."

The call from the mountain must lead us upstream, or gravity will take us to the ocean. Our response to the Golden Rule is the determining factor. "Friends, I would like to introduce you to....."

What's New?

Little did we dream the Mississippi River would get so low that barge traffic would come to a halt. Neither did we realize that the highly criticized Tennessee-Tombigbee Waterway would become the life-line alternative. In the drought of 1988, we have learned again, "Never Say Never". It is a lesson we can bring to the Church---valuing the proven, but adding the new.

Lyle Schaller writes in the September issue of <u>Net-Results</u> about the "Biomarkers of Church Growth". His formula for determining if a congregation is "programming for Church Growth" is: membership (501), minus the last two numbers (01), which leaves (5). The question is, "Does the number of adult face-to-face groups organized in the last twenty-four months equal or exceed that number?". Our number is five.

The following short term and long term groups have been added at First Christian Church in the last twenty months:

1. Bethany Sunday School Class
2. Young Women's Bible Study
3. Musical "Cool in the Furnace"
4. Senior Adult Trips:
    Circus, "Carousel", River Cruise, "Passion Play", "South Pacific", Folk Center Foliage Trip to Mountain View, Christmas Tour at Marlgate Plantation.
5. Musical "Down by the Creek Bank"
6. Class on Beliefs and practices
7. Wednesday Spiritual Growth Classes
8. Church Growth Panel
9. Terrific Tuesdays in July
10. Super-Kids
11. Lively Learners and Cherub Church
12. Children's Sermon 1st Sundays
13. Adult Education Series Sunday Evenings
14. Firm Believers Exercise Class
15. Broadway Spectacular I
16. Broadway Spectacular II
17. 1st Annual Basketball Classic
18. Tuesday Night Basketball
19. Minister's Welcome Class
20. Sunday Evening 2-5 Year Olds Group
21. Nursery Committee

First Christian Church is programming for Church Growth through new groups, activities, and ministries. These groups are "Ports of Entry". Let us keep the channels clear and ports of entry abundant with friendly and caring receptions to all who may find haven in the harbors of refuge from the storms or droughts of life.

Light and Shadow

On a rainy Saturday morning, I watched a painter on television mix light and dark colors on his palette. As he brushed the contrasting colors on the canvas he said, "light and shadow, light and shadow". Gradually his picture took its final form of beauty. If it was all shadow, it would have been dreary. If it was all light, it would have been boring. The final beauty was in the blend of light and shadow. That is the true form of life. It is our faith in Christ that sustains us in the blending of the joys and sorrows of life. It is the wisdom of God and nature of the church family that Paul describes when he says, "rejoicing with those who rejoice and weeping with those who weep". Let us thank God that Christ is faithful to sustain us both in the light and the shadow, our joys and sorrows. The beauty of the finished picture will be by the touch of His loving hand. Until then, O Lord, blend the colors of our lives that the beauty of Your love may be seen in us. Amen.

This is the Place

There is something about human nature that seeks a sign from God at the crossroads of life. Lord, am I making the right decision? Is this where you want me to be at this time, Lord?

Gideon asked God to give him a sign if he was to be His instrument. He laid out a fleece on the threshing floor and asked that the fleece be wet and the ground be dry. Not yet sure he changed the order a second time, the ground wet and the fleece dry. He sought a double sign, and in reverse. (Judges 6:36)

Jesus said, "This generation seeks a sign", needing some strange phenomena or alteration in the laws of nature to convince us to act, go, or do. Jesus calls us to live by faith, not by signs. We are to listen for God's word, be open to His leading, prompted by the inner Spirit and the still small voice within.

There has been no "sign" about our coming to Little Rock. It has been on faith and at the leading of God. Sunday, the confirmation came from within. As Eric Chu played the violin during communion, there was a welling up of the Spirit of God within my heart, and an inner conviction of "this is the place God wants us to be". In that I rejoice. "Lead on, O King Eternal."

Chapter 9
What's In A Name

What's in a Name?

Someone commented one day that when they drove through the country, they felt they had taken a cheap trip to the Holy Land. Having a proper church name is obviously important. Lean back, look out the window, and enjoy the sites.

Ahead is Mount Sinai Baptist Church. That is where Moses received the 10 commandments from God. Canaan Presbyterian Church is down the road, just beyond Salem Church of Christ. Mount Moriah Methodist Church is an old altar site, brush arbor meeting place. Bethany Christian Church is further west, where Jesus met some of his favorite people and rested in their home. These are "right site" churches.

A second grouping of church names emphasized "right doctrine and relationships". There is New Hope Cumberland Presbyterian Church, Our Redeemer Lutheran Church, Good Shepherd Lutheran Church, Grace Episcopal Church, Trinity Episcopal Church, St. Joseph's Catholic Church, St. Paul African Methodist Episcopal Church, St. Bartholomew's Episcopal Church, Faith Tabernacle, Christ's Chapel, etc. Then there is that category of numerical distinction like: First Christian, First Methodist, First Presbyterian, First Baptist, etc.

Is it possible to get all the Biblical, Doctrinal, and site content in a church name? Here is a near perfect try:

First, Apostolic, Trinitarian, New Jerusalem, Charismatic, Born Again, Inclusive, New Union, Independent, Cooperative, Fundamental, Progressive, Holy Catholic, One Savior, Full Gospel, Four Square, Open Door, Sacred Bible Church.

But, no doubt, there will be at least one person who will not agree on this fine effort to name a church. Well, one more attempt, but it may be too simple for anyone to take seriously. "And in Antioch the disciples were for the first time called Christians." (Acts 11:26)

Check the luggage racks for your personal items. Watch your step. Tomorrow we go to Antioch.

Andy Was a Dandy

Very little is known about Andrew in the Scripture. Yet, he was one of the most influential disciples, whose work reaches through the centuries. He was a fisherman. He owned a house with his brother at Capernaum. He was a disciple of Jesus. John says of Andrew, "He first found his brother Simon Peter and said, 'We have found the Christ.' He brought him to Jesus." (John 1:40-42) It was Peter who made the good confession in Matthew 16. Peter stood up on Pentecost and preached when 3,000 were added to the Church. But, it was Andrew who brought Peter to Christ.

Beloved, one of the most important things we can do for Christ is to invite our brothers and sisters, mothers and fathers, children and grandchildren, neighbors, friends, business associates, and fellow workers to church, Sunday School, a fellowship meal, Vacation Bible School, etc. The mission field is not only the other side of the world; it is going to be where we are today. Let us covenant to be more like Andrew, "who found his brother and brought him to Christ". The most important person in church is <u>you</u>. God has some work for each of us to do. May each of us find it.

The Gift of Work
Genesis 1:26-31   Ephesians 2:1-10

And God blessed them and said to them, "Be fruitful and multiply, and fill the earth and subdue it; and have dominion over the fish of the sea and over the birds of the air and over every thing that moves on the earth."

Labor Day Sunday

Across the street, workers are building an addition to Collier Library at the University of North Alabama. It is a marvel to behold, and the little boy in me is still spellbound at workers doing construction. I have seen the surveyors, excavators, carpenters, steel workers, brick masons, electricians, plumbers, and a host of others working in the extremes of heat or cold and dangerous heights. There is an invisible army supporting them with materials, food, engineering, financing, and transportation. In addition to the skills, there is a harmony of workmanship suited to the right time and place.

One day, that building will be filled with books, magazines, and papers—the works of authors, writers, publishers, secretaries, woodcutters, paper makers, truckers, etc. Teachers will work with students. The students will work toward an education that will permit them to learn a skill through which they then can support themselves, and contribute toward the well being of others.

On Labor Day, we pay tribute to workers who enrich our lives; but especially do we thank God, who created us with the capacity of creativity, hard work, harmony, and endurance. Worship is a celebration of work completed, and anticipation of work to do:

> "So God blessed the seventh day and hallowed it, because on it God rested from all his work which he had done in creation."
> (Genesis 2: 3)

Giving a Father's Blessing

(from the Father's Day Sermon, June 20, 1993)

Being a man and learning how to give a father's blessing is an ongoing process. Yet, I think there are some basics that are not culturally conditioned, but are valid imperatives, which are timeless. Biological and Spiritual fathers are a part of God's plan in Giving the Blessing to Children. Here are seven ways to give a father's blessing.

1. Expect a child to be a blessing. "Joseph is a fruitful vine, near a

2. Model strength with flexibility. "They shot at him with hostility, but his bow remained steady, and his strong arms stayed limber." (Genesis 49:24)
3. Teach children how to look for spiritual treasure. "With blessings of the heavens above and deep below." (Genesis 49:25)
4. Display a daily trust in our Heavenly Father. "Because of your father's God who helps you." (Genesis 49:25)
5. Scatter the seed of blessing generously. "Fathers, do not exasperate your children; instead, bring them up in the training and instruction of the Lord." (Ephesians 6:4)
6. Maintain a refreshing attitude. "I was glad when Stephanas, Fortunatas and Achaicus arrived, because they supplied what was lacking from you." (I Corinthians 16:17)
7. Placing great value on giving a father's blessing. "Your father's blessings are greater than the blessings of the ancient mountains, than the bounty of the age old hills. (Genesis 49:26)

When Jacob gave the blessing to the children of Israel, he raised their vision from the bondage of the present to the promise of the future. Every child, every home, every community, every society, and every nation is enriched when Godly men give the blessing. When "See you Sunday" comes true for more men, then more dreams will come true.

Seven Portraits

Several of you have given me an article called "The Church". Some of you commented, "Bob, this is about a generation that left the church, and a generation that is finding its way back. The scene today is for the church to become a "seeker of seekers". The exit of a generation from the church left great change, a survivor mentality. Many congregations have been left mortally wounded—"gut shot". Dazed, there is a search for strength in making camp with other wounded and dying pilgrims. Water is rationed, bread is scarce, and the strong are asked to break out the rations.

The next sermon series, "Seven Portraits of the Bride of Christ" will look to the Church growing in faith, and centering life around Christ.

FIRST LOVE- "Yet I hold this against you; you have forsaken your first love. (Revelation 2:4)

TREASURING TRUE RICHES- "I know your afflictions and your poverty—yet you are rich." (Revelation 2"4)

THE BREAD OF SOUND TEACHING- "I have a few things against you: you have people there who hold to the teaching of Balaam."
(Revelation 2:14)

HOLDING UP AND HOLDING ON- "only hold on to what you have until I come...I will also give him the morning star." (Revelation 2:14)

REPUTATION OF PACE SETTING- "I know your deeds; you have a reputation of being alive, but you are dead." (Revelation 3:1)

EMBRACING THE OPEN DOOR- I have placed before you an open door that no one can shut." (Revelation 3:8)

COMMITTED WITH PASSION- "I wish you were one or the other."
   (Revelation 3:15)

I invite you to join me as we go to the mirror and see Seven Portraits of the Bride of Christ.

A Winning Strategy

In 1980, I visited another church in another state while attending a Bible Training Workshop. I walked in off the street and did not know a single person in that congregation. It was a large church with two worship services and a membership of 5,000. The first person to spot me was one of the ministers. He introduced himself and welcomed me. It was coffee hour in the fellowship hall, and I walked into a sea of new faces. No one greeted me or introduced themselves or asked who I was or sought any personal information. It was obvious they were a friendly congregation, for they were busy talking to each other, smiling, laughing, sharing news, and making plans.

My strategy was to let them make the first move. I stood in one place for five minutes and sipped coffee. Then I slowly changed positions, staying a few feet away from a happy chatting group. There were a few glances my way, but no initiative. Finally, I moved on to the sanctuary and took my seat for the worship service. It was a beautiful service in a beautiful place. After the benediction, I slipped out the door just as successfully as I had slipped in –waiting for someone else to make the first move.

That experience taught me two things about what makes a friendly church: First, friends greet friends; Second, friendly people make new friends. If I don't do both, I am only half as friendly as I think I am. There is a wise saying, "To have a friend, be a friend".

It thrills me to see a genuine friendliness in First Christian Church. God is using it to His Glory.

Papa's Gold Watch

There is an art to "stepping down" that is best triggered by the ticking of the inner clock. Judge Henry Woods at age 72, and after years of court battles, heard the inner chimes. Whitey Herzog listened to the inner chambers of his feelings as the St. Louis Cardinals dropped below the level of Pride's tolerance, and Whitey said, "I am out of here."

Gunther Williams, my hero, also 55 years old, is making his farewell tour as the world's greatest animal trainer with Ringling Brothers and Barnum & Bailey Circus. Gunther said he had not had a day off for 20 years as elephants, tigers, and horses compelled him to consistently present himself every day to maintain pride, life and limb. Gunther's inner clock said in the prime of health and success, "shift your talents backstage while you are in charge instead of the circus being in charge of you."

In ministry, we may be long overdue for some new models of "stepping up" and "stepping down". One day, 10 years down the road or before, I will hear my inner clock say "now!" Until then, I must reflect. During the '80's our churches declined. In the '90's we are dedicated to "developing dynamic, vital congregations with dynamic faith communities". Recent figures indicate 45% of our ministers will be retiring in the next 10 years. We need a new model for "stepping up" and "stepping down". There is an "ice floe mentality" that has frozen many of our churches. It happens when a church won't move and a minister won't move. The result is declining congregations. When both move, our churches will grow again. It is no longer acceptable to stay with a church 'til it melts and then jump to another one, like an ice floe. Being faithful can mean leaving as well as staying.

What is important is to feel excited about ministry, witness, and fourfold growth: in numbers, spirituality, stewardship, and compassion. No work can be more exciting than ministry. My father gave me grandfather's pocket watch in 1955 when I accepted my first student pastorate at Newbern, Tennessee. I already have the gold watch. What keeps me excited is the golden opportunities of this church. I rejoice that we both are growing.

Voices from the Past

Prudence compels us to judge the difference of behavior for fun, profit, or both. My first earnings were from picking strawberries, paying five cents a quart. After picking a 24 quart crate, I gathered my pay and headed for the Annual Strawberry Festival Carnival. As I held my $1.20 in hand, at the gate my father's parting words were: "Son, remember you are here for fun, and these folks are here for profit."

I was magnetically drawn to the dragline machines; glass cages piled with nickels, quarters, and silver dollars. For five cents you could operate a dragline by hand and go for riches. The operator beckoned, "Son, try your skill." I lost more nickels than I caught. Sometimes I still hear my father's voice, "Son, remember you are here for fun, and these folks are here for profit."

Miss Byrd was a delightful lady in my first church. In her 70's she was jovial, frugal, and wise. On visits to her house, I might find her on the house repairing the roof, or up in a pear tree picking pears. Passing on her frugal philosophy to me she said, "Son, take care of the dimes and the dollars will take care of themselves." I immediately went to the Ben Franklin Variety Store and purchased a metal bank for dimes. Gradually I accumulated $100.00. An old high school friend came by with a deal for a new business. I bought $100.00 worth of stock. Once they sent me a check for $14.90. Five years ago, I called to learn my investment ran out of steam out west, and disappeared. I heard again the frugal voice, "Son, take care of the dimes and the dollars will take care of themselves."

After two years in Arkansas, I decided to taste the flavor of Hot Springs, and accepted the invitation of a friend to go to the races. Good counsel was offered, "Son, take twenty dollars you can afford to lose." I came home with $1.80, and the conviction that my fortune was not in Hot Springs. I heard voices again.

Preparing for Hummingbirds

A friend gave us a beautiful bright red hummingbird feeder. I am thinking about filling it with sweet sugar water, adding some red food color, and waiting for the hummingbirds to find it. I've made sure the hot sun will not ferment the water, and that bees, ants, and varmints can't reach it. It is hanging high in the storage room behind two doors. Hummingbirds that can't find such a treasure don't deserve it.

Net Results, a motivational magazine for evangelism and church vitality, list six characteristics of churches that attract adults under age forty:

1. A faster-paced, more meaningful worship experience.
2. Strong music and choir programs for all age groups.
3. Extensive adult Bible study programs.
4. An aggressive evangelism program.
5. A pastor who has an attractive personality, preaches well, is productive, and takes initiative in leading.
6. High expectations regarding financial and time commitment from members.

Net Results, June 1990

On second thought, I am going to place that hummingbird feeder outside, toward the sun, among the flowers and crape myrtles. I will make it vulnerable to make it available. After all, I don't have the only hummingbird feeder in town, and I want to see hummingbirds. They are one of the wonders of God.

The Cross and the Crown

The last week in the life of Christ confronts us with the extremes of life, the cross of suffering, and the crown of victory. Easter, resurrection morning, means very little without the darkness of a mother's grief, a betraying friend, a denying disciple, confused followers, and cruelty on the cross accompanied by disheartening humiliation.

There is no way to leap from the applause of Palm Sunday to the angel's good news to early rising tomb visitors, "He is not here; for he has risen, as he said. Come, see the place where he lay." (Matthew 28:6) Walking with Jesus during his last week is in many ways parallel to our dark nights of the soul when we, too, "walk through the valley of the shadow of death."

Easter is God's triumphant answer to the valley of hurt, injustice, corruption, betrayal, cruelty, disappointment, and death. God speaks to more than just the "Monday Blues". He addresses the two big sinkholes of life: the repercussions of sin, and the finality of death. To leap from Palm Sunday to Easter Sunday is to skip the doubting questions that magnify God's encouraging answer at the empty tomb. May our daily troubles and doubts prepare us to receive God's good news in the resurrection of Christ.

A Trail of Rose Petals

The sermon Sunday on procrastination incubated from a poem shared by Mary Sue Johnson. The poem spoke of sharing roses with those you love while they can enjoy them.

In my ministry, I often follow a trail of rose petals. Roses are left on my desk. Flowers are sent to our home. Sometimes we find buckets of flowers in the church kitchen before a birthday party, reception, or dinner. Sometimes there is a trail of rose petals down the hall of the nursing home or in the hospital rooms. Vases and cans of fresh roses may pop up in most any home, and fresh flowers in our worship services. Frequently, they are from the gardens of Mary Sue Johnson, and Wilder and Sue Jolly Watts.

Growing flowers may be a hobby, but sharing them is a way of life. There are so many things we can do to brighten the lives of others: a smile, a card, a note, a phone call, soup, candy, brownies, taking time for a greeting, paying a debt—or forgiving one, a thank you, or word of encouragement—or a rose.

When it comes to life and love, we can't afford to wait too long. There are a million ways to show Christian love... today.

I am looking for the crocus. God sends it each year after the cold winter to say, "I love you. Prepare your gardens."

An Example is Where You Find It

The young people led us in a beautiful service of worship Sunday. We thank God for each one. Youth have an immeasurable influence on our lives.

Paul writes to the young preacher, Timothy, "Let no one despise your youth, but set the believers an example in speech and conduct, in love, in faith, in purity." (I Timothy 4:12) Youth may be a reason for some poor decisions but never an excuse. Paul believed a good example was where you found it.

One of the joys of those who work with youth (whether parent, teacher, or friend) is to see their progress. We are blessed in the church with the opportunity to see growth and development in faith, leadership, and service over a period of years, and even a lifetime.

We thank God when the fed become feeders, and the led become leaders, as admonished in I Timothy 4:15, "Practice these duties, devote yourself to them, so that all may see your progress."

And what is our goal? "Rather, speaking the truth in love, we are to grow up in every way into him who is the head, into Christ." (Ephesians 4:15) Following Christ is not a matter of age, but devotion.

The Walking Bible

He was called "the walking Bible." Brother Perry was the long time pastor of a rural congregation. He and Mrs. Perry lived in a gold fish bowl in the little community. Strangely, some people knew what he had for breakfast, even though his house was not bugged; yet, he was unashamed of scrambled eggs and biscuits.

One did not call Brother Perry's prayer line. He was the prayer line. He dropped by when there was an illness. He stayed up nights waiting with families as the death angel tarried. He stopped daily at the country store to gather news, and chatted at the cotton gin with tired but rejoicing harvesters. He was a presence whose name you not only knew, but he knew yours. He was there.

He could not tell you how to contribute to the ministry with a Visa card. He was known far and wide, not because he was always asking, but because he was forever giving. His car was a tool, not a luxury.

Many of the members who filled the churches in the cities came from his congregation at the crossroads. They made the city churches stronger. Thank God for the Brother Perrys, servants of God, who not only talk the Bible, but live it. For "a good name is better to be chosen than great riches, and loving favor above silver and gold." (Proverbs 22:1)

Lord, forgive us for confusing entertainment with commitment.

Here Comes Miss Hettie

Ministers should be required to take a class in Organizing Christmas Parades 102. It would fit in well between Drink Machine 101 and Sanctuary Temperatures 103.

Putting together a Christmas Parade must be a real challenge. Let's be fair. All the entries will take a number and you will appear in the order of your draw. No problem with that... 1, 2, 3, 4, 5... Barney Fyfe style.

But nothing could be so simple. The Girl Scouts will not walk in front of the men speeding in the little cars. The Flag Corps wants a fair distance from the islander-clad fraternity. The churches and merchants discuss whether the manger scene or Santa floats should be first or last. The bands refuse to march behind the horses. So, the numerical sequence gives way to priority of need. Hopefully, order is established on the basis of concern and Christian Love. IT IS A CHRISTMAS PARADE.

Out of the blue, like Zorro, appears Miss Hettie. She is not the ghost of Christmas Past, but the Spirit of Christmas, disguised somewhat. She wears a knotted wool cap on her head, and a knee-length coat of some ancient vintage. She wears tennis shoes and gym socks, for she came to march. She marches beside the band, struts with the majorettes, drops back to the scouts, joins another band, and brings up the rear with the horses.

When the crowd, leaning into the street, shouts, "Here comes Miss Hettie!" some will think of Murphy's Law. Others will think of the Spirit of Christ. To see her excitement makes one a little embarrassed at the sight of idle feet.

Jesus said, "But to what shall I compare this generation? It is like children sitting in the market places and calling to their playmates,
>"We piped to you, and you did not dance;
>We wailed, and you did not mourn."
>   (Matthew 11:16-17)

Lord, forgive us of our mean moods. Wait up, Miss Hettie.

Blind Spots

Crossing a one-way street should be no problem, especially when not over a car a minute passes during rush hour. The way seemed perfectly clear. Suddenly, there was a blue Ford appearing out of nowhere on a collision course with Mr. B. Careful. A disaster was avoided by careful maneuvering. The only explanation for the sudden appearance was a "blind spot" in the eye of the driver, windshield of the car, or both. Blind spots can be disastrous.

How much scripture are we blind to seeing? There are 66 books of the Bible—39 in the Old Testament, and 27 in the New Testament. Do we only read the New Testament, since we are a New Testament People? Or, is the Old Testament a preparation for grasping the depth of the New? Someone said they only used a red-letter edition of the Bible and read only the words of Jesus printed in red. How can we avoid scriptural blind spots? The 66 books of the Bible are progressive revelation. W.O. Lappin used to say to his college class, "The more you understand of the Old Testament, the more you will understand of the New."

One way to avoid scriptural blind spots in the eye of the preacher and church is by following the selected readings of scripture from the Lectionary. In 1978, representatives of 13 churches made proposals to achieve consensus in the scripture readings in worship within three year cycles. A recovery of the ancient practice of relating scripture and worship gives momentum to the praise of God across denominational lines. This helps the preacher avoid reading or preaching only on his favorite passages and forms the discipline of ordering worship toward seeking "the whole counsel of God."

Four passages are suggested weekly. This week they are:

Psalm 24, Genesis 4:3-10, Mark 5:21-43, II Corinthians 8:7-15

The Psalm is used in the call to worship. After reading the scripture, study and prayer, a passage for the sermon is chosen by Wednesday. Rather than bring a topic to the text, God is given the opportunity to speak His message through the scripture. We have been following the discipline of the Lectionary since January 1985. May God help us with our blind spot, and enable us to see the beauty of His Holiness in both Word and Worship, as Paul says in I Corinthians 14:40, "but all things should be done decently and in order."

"Hello, Anybody Home?"

The humidity was 85%, and "it rained cats and dogs." The air was so thick you could hardly breathe. The skin was clammy, and a fresh shirt hung on the shoulders like Monday morning laundry on a pasture fence. On those high humidity days, one dreams of moving to Arizona or surrendering to air-conditioned imprisonment.

High humility makes one about as miserable as high humidity, when humility is mistaken for passivity. "Where do you want to go on vacation this year?" "Oh, anywhere." "Let's go out for dinner. What are you hungry for?" "Oh, you name it." "Well, what do you think?" "Oh, what do you think?" At this point, one wonders if anybody is home. Check the mailbox. See if there are papers in the yard. Ask a neighbor if they are on vacation. Break a window and check for gas fumes.

Consider Boomer, the dog, and Sam, the cat. The kennel owners vowed that cats were just as smart as dogs, maybe smarter. "Good morning, Sam." Sam just sits. No change in facial expression. He muses on every thought and feeling without returning any intelligent sign of life, friendship, or interest. Boomer runs through the yard, barks a hello, wags his tail at a mere smile, turns flips for a piece of sweet roll, and lets his air-conditioning run with mouth open and tongue dripping.

Jesus praised humility, but not passivity. While he said, "Blessed are the meek, for they shall inherit the earth" (Matthew 5:5), he also said, "You will know them by their fruits." (Matthew 7:16)

Sam will keep his feline secrets intact. No one will ever know how smart he really is. He's a cool cat. "Boomer, stop licking my hand. Get your canine nose out of my face. You rascal, you!" Boomer may not be the smartest, but who cares? He will never be mistaken for a cushion.

The Wave

There is a difference in creating waves and waiting for waves. Would-be surfers splash optimism as they swim toward the hope of a good ride. Treading water beside their surfboards, they scan the horizon for a wave with promise. They do not create waves, but hitchhike, taking what comes, doing the best they can, signing each ride with the personal signature of praise or ridicule, based on performance.

The Wave Pool lures thousands who demand big thrills at low risk. No need to wait for the ocean to burp. A giant pump and a timer faithfully produce waves. The only thing to watch is the watch. As faithful as "Old Faithful." There she goes. On to the rafts... ride, bounce, and buck. Then the waves subside and the surfers are back where they started... "much ado about nothing."

Then, there is "The Wave" in Busch Stadium. Only God knows how it started. Maybe a Redbird burped, or a fan. It came rolling like a giant tidal wave. Survivors—29,257 ticket holders, leaping to their feet on its crest, and after shouting with raised arms, fell back into their seats to watch it circumvent the stadium three more times. What a mighty force generated by different people deciding to do the same thing toward a harmonious end.

What a thrill to be a part of "The Wave" in the Church. Individuals creating waves for good: raising budgets, supporting Christian education in Sunday School Classes and bible study, working with other denominations in the Help Center, Horizons, Safeplace, Attention Homes and Grace Mountain Home, visiting the sick, counseling the troubled, ministering to the bereaved, seeking the lost, praising God in worship, being a force with God's Force for good in Regional and General Church.

Paul writes in I Corinthians 12:27, "Now you are the body of Christ, and individually members of it."

Sometimes we are tempted to just wait for good waves to appear, or only ride low risk, no place waves. God calls us to unite in creating Waves that touch the shores of the world with the good news of God's love in Christ.

"Don't go near the water till you learn to swim" is ironical advice to would-be surfers.

Monday Night at Busch Stadium

After two and a half days and nights of church meetings at the General Board in St. Louis last week, we took Monday night for relaxation and went to Bush Stadium to see the St. Louis Cardinals and San Diego Padres baseball game.

Without a doubt, baseball fans must be as persevering as baseball players. The hardships are many for the fans, and it is a wonder they can maintain high levels of interest and commitment.

The parking was awful, in a poorly lighted area, at a rip-off price of $3.00, and we were forced to cross a major traffic artery. Not a single person out of 29,276 fans, outside our party, spoke a friendly greeting, or gave a warm smile. The seat was metal, and had no cushion. They sold the programs. The food was overpriced. My bag of parched peanuts cost 80 cents—4 cents per peanut. No Cardinal has called.

The singing was "the pits". You would think American citizens would know the National Anthem, or could read the giant video screen. Midway in the game, a fight broke out behind us... high school seniors on their senior trip. The whole party was escorted out. After the game, two women in front of us brawled. Someone said one had spilled beer on the other.

It was an exciting night for my first professional baseball game... all more than I had fantasized as a West Tennessee youth through the radio voice of Harry Carey. I definitely hope to go again. Next time, I think I will watch the game.

The Psalmist said, "I was glad when they said to me, 'Let us go to the house of the Lord.'" (Psalm 122:1) In the long run, the Lord's business may prove more relaxing than the world's business.

God Bless the Children

It is the wisdom of God that He came to the world in the form of a child. He came in innocence and simplicity. He surrounded us with the beauty of infancy and possibility.

Simeon was one of the first to recognize the brilliance of God's gift in a baby:

"He took him up in his arms and blessed God and said, 'Lord, now lettest thou thy servant depart in peace, according to thy word; for mine eyes have seen thy salvation which thou has prepared in the presence of all peoples, a light for the Gentiles, and for glory to thy people Israel.'" (Luke 2:28-32)

It is no surprise that children are wide-eyed in wonder at Christmas. They are pilgrims of possibilities looking for Bethlehem's Star, seeking a light they can follow throughout a lifetime. Grown-ups are busy with pageantry and nativity, for those who have stumbled know how important it is to follow a worthy star.

Thank God for children who never let us forget the sheer beauty of innocence. Bless the children who present dandelion flowers as gifts, the first fruits of the morning. Bless the children who give hugs, and drive away the chill of loneliness. Bless children who greet us by name, who remind us that in their eyes we are somebody. Bless the children who carry "Going to Grandma's" luggage, for they hold the keys to happy hearts. Bless the children, who by confession of faith and baptism, become bothers and sisters with saints everywhere.

Thank God for His children of all ages, for they have learned to say, "Our Father, who art in heaven, hallowed be thy name. Thy kingdom come. Thy will be done, on earth as it is in heaven." (Matthew 6:9-10)

Thank God for the gift of children, and for the gift of the Christ-child. Good morning, world! There is crying in the cradle.

Chapter 10
Who Will Say The Blessing

Who Will Say the Blessing?

My sermon series for the month of May is "Who will say the blessing?" When we gather as a family, different people say the blessings. If there is one meal, we call on one person. If there several meals, we call on different people to say the blessing. As Dad, I usually begin with the first blessing, and as we gather again and again, I ask, "Who will say the blessing?"

In the church family, we remember the blessings of our mothers, grandmothers, and all the women who have mothered us over the years. Mothers give us birth. It is the precious gift of life. Mothers teach us, help us, nurture us, forgive us, feed us, clean up our messes, dress us, pick up after us. Yes, Dads are helpers, too. Mother calls, writes, answers the phone, and says, "I am going to tell your father." Thank you, Moms.

May 17 is Youth Sunday at Madison Christian Church. How blessed we are to have children and youth at Church. We have teachers and leaders for children. In each service there is a Young Disciple's Moment. There is Worship and Wonder to teach the Bible and love for God. We have Youth meetings. The youth will be participating in the MANNA Programs on Wednesday evenings, and helping with Set-Up and Cleanup on May 20. We are excited to know, see, and experience our Next Generation. God is good.

King David is credited with a lovely thanksgiving psalm about "Who will say the Blessing? (Psalm 103:1-5)

"Praise the Lord, O my soul; all my inmost being praise his holy name.
Praise the Lord, O my soul, and forget not all his benefits—Who forgives all your sins and heals all your diseases,
Who redeems your life from the pit and crowns you with love and compassion,
Who satisfies your desires with good things so your youth is renewed like the eagle's.

Who will say the blessing? Jesus taught us all how to be a blessing in Matthew 5:1-16. In fact, being a blessing is saying the blessing. In Christ, we do both. "We will..."

Pastoral Leadership is...

Pastoral leadership is listening. One of my friends said, "Bob, you need to attend the Church Evangelism Workshops before the General Assembly." I thought, "Why should I listen to him? He is a young minister. He was in the senior class of high school conference when I was a director at Hargis. I have been to Bible College and graduated from Seminary. What does he know that I don't know?" I did take his kind and friendly input, and he was right. Herb Miller led this emphasis on helping our pastors learn how to grow a church by reaching people. For years I never missed one of the NEW meetings, and heard many outstanding ministers from different denominations. I brought home tapes, and shared them. I learned to listen to the wisdom of colleagues and teachers.

Pastoral leadership is reading. My ministry took an upward trend with an inward change after I read a book by Stephen Covey. Dr. Covey has led me in a progressive direction in pastoral leadership in cultivating good habits. One improvement was using a flip chart and printing a minister's report for church cabinet and board meetings. The chart will show where you have been, what you have done, how you are planning your goals, along with achievements. This is proactive instead of becoming defensive when someone questions your performance and agenda. You show leadership instead of asking what the church wants to do next.

Pastoral leadership is utilizing the church paper. The larger the church, the more you will hear "Communication is the Key". In the smaller church, everybody knows who goes where, what they had for breakfast, and who is puny, sick, or having surgery. The bigger the church, the more you'll hear, "I didn't know that." One of the NEA (National Evangelism Association) workshops was about the communication of the minister in the church letter. I learned to write an article every week, about fifty articles a year, front page focused on pastoral planning, affirmations, sermon subjects, and upcoming events. Seldom did I focus on yesterday... The focus was on the present and future. Congratulations were appropriate.

Pastoral leadership is "When Bottom Line Is Tops". Why follow the wrong crowd? Take initiative. Sometimes you walk with a group. Sometimes you walk in another direction. What is important is to walk toward the next chapter, where you feel God is leading you. This chapter of my book is devoted to articles from numerous church papers over the years. It is my example of pastoral leadership in the Practice of Ministry. With these articles, visitors, shut-ins, friends, family, and the congregation felt in touch with me. And in these pastoral articles, I felt in touch with God, Christ's Church, the leading of the Holy Spirit, and pastoral leadership. "And that's all I got to say about that," said Forrest Gump.

Who are the Stegalls?

Bob was born on the farm at Humboldt, Tennessee, son of Clark and Louise Stegall. He accepted the call to Christian ministry at Central Avenue Christian Church, was ordained by the Tennessee Region of the Christian Church (Disciples of Christ) in 1966. He is a graduate of Johnson Bible College, Vanderbilt Divinity School, and earned his Doctor of Ministry Degree from Lexington Theological Seminary in 1978. He was a minister at First Christian Church, Florence, Alabama for 18 years, and retired as Senior Minister of First Christian Church, Little Rock, Arkansas in 1997. He is married to Kay Frances Ward, his high school sweetheart.

Kay graduated from the University of North Alabama. She was office manager for a medical practice for 9 years in Little Rock, Renal Associates. She worked for a dermatologist in Florence, Alabama for 9 years, and retired in May 2006. She is a trained teacher of the Bethel Bible Series. She has led Women's Retreats, and served as a group leader with Christian Women's Fellowship Retreats. Kay was elected Moderator of the Christian Church in Alabama-Northwest Florida in 2010.

Bob and Kay moved back to Alabama in 1997 to be near their family, fish, host fish fries, enjoy friendships, and do interim ministries. They have 3 children: Pat, band director, Maryjane, kindergarten teacher, and Jennifer, registered nurse. The grandchildren are: Justin, Chris, Kevin, and Caroline.

The Stegalls completed their 11th interim ministry. Bob is past president of the Tuscumbia Civitan Club, and past chaplain of District 8 in Alabama North Civitan International. Bob has served as president of the Davis Estates Homeowners Association, where they built their dream home, "Greenbo" in 1997.

My Best Friend and Soul Mate

Kay Frances Ward Stegall is my best friend and soul mate. She is my high school sweetheart, beloved of fifty-five years and mother of our three children. We met on a Humboldt High School trip to the Mid-South Fair in Memphis, Tennessee. It was a joint trip of the FHA (Future Homemakers of America) and the FFA (Future Farmers of America). We rode on a school bus. I sat with my friend, Joe Sanford. At the Fair we saw Kay and her friends. Joe said, "Bobby, this is my cousin, Kay Ward." We said hello and I invited her to go to see the Butterfly exhibit and rodeo with me. We rode back to Humboldt sitting together on the bus. We sat on the back seat. We have been together ever since and most of the time sitting on the front seat. Sometimes we get to church early and can sit on the back seat again.

Kay became the President of the FHA. She was chosen to receive the Betty Crocker of the Year Award. We were married and she joined me at Johnson Bible College in my senior year where our son, Pat was born. Kay wanted to be a stay at home mom to devote her life being with our children. At our first church we served, Bells, Tennessee, our second child, Mary Jane was born. Kay was a good manager of our household expenses and we lived within $3,600 a year salary. After four years, we moved to Springfield, Tennessee so I could attend seminary at Vanderbilt, and our third child, Jennifer Diane, was born. Our three children loved being with their mother every day.

    Kay grew up in a banker's family. Her mother, Frances, and Aunt Nana, worked at Merchant's State Bank. Her "Uncle Honey", Mr. George, was the president of the bank. Sometimes the family would be late for dinner. They called and said, "The auditors showed up today. We are trying to balance the books." Kay has always been a good manager of money. We have negotiated our purchases and stayed within our budget. At the first of the month our bank statements arrive. Kay looks for the pennies and makes sure everything balances in her account. I look at our account to make sure enough is there to cover all the bases. No, we don't fight over money. We even pay each other back when we borrow. When money is the second reason for disputes among spouses we will avoid that brick in the road. "Here, darling, is the quarter I borrowed." "Thank you, sweetie. You are my heartbeat." There, we have avoided the first reason, too.

    Serving in the church is one of Kay's passions. She

has given devotions, preached on special days, led CWF (Christian Women's Fellowship) retreats, written for devotional booklets, attended as a voting delegate at the General Assemblies, helped begin new Sunday School Classes, taught the Bethel Bible Series and Through the Bible in a Year Bible Studies, served as Choir Director, taught line dancing, created plays and programs for church fellowship events. Presently, she is writing a script to introduce the Andy Griffith Bible Study, and teaches The Parables of Jesus Sunday School Class. She is also Moderator-Elect of the Christian Church (Disciples of Christ) in Alabama Northwest Florida. Together, we have served in 11 interim ministries, and led the Senior Adult Retreat. We are scheduled to participate in the Minister's and Mate's Retreat, sharing about Leaving a Church Healthy and Happy.

    Kay graduated Magna Cum Laude from the University of North Alabama in 1980 with degrees in English and Music. She sang a solo in the Christmas Cantata, Handel's Messiah. She has helped with church tours to Israel, Greece and Turkey. She has worked in the offices of five doctors, and retired as Office Manager for Renal Specialists. She was invited to come back to work after she retired, and she worked nine more years for Dr. Bennett, Dermatologist. At numerous fish fries hosted in our home for churches, groups and friends, Kay earned the well deserved reputation of "The Hush Puppy Queen'. She was elected to serve as secretary of the Tuscumbia Civitan Club, and a voting Delegate to the International Convention in Las Vegas, where her father, Ernest Ward lived for several years.

    Kay was presented the Honored Minister's Spouse Award on December 2, 2007 at First Christian

Church, Huntsville, Alabama by John Mobley, Regional Minister. Kay and Bob were recognized for fifty years of ministry. John said it was the first time he had presented an "Honored Minister's Spouse" award, and he included the scripture, "Well done, good and faithful servant," Matthew 25:21

In 2008, Kay was presented the "Woman of Compassion Award" by the Florence, Alabama Ladies Pilot Club. After a trip with First Christian Church, Florence, Alabama to the St. Jude Hospital for Children in Memphis, Kay helped organize a group of women who sewed blankets, clothes and tote bags for families with patients at the hospital. Sandra Vetters, president of the Pilot Club presented the award.

September 24, 2009, Kay and her husband, Bob, were presented the Tuscumbia Civitan Club "Civitan of the Year Award." Kay served as secretary for two years. She cooked and served food to the club on the first Thursday of the month for a year. She became famous for her brownies and chocolate chip cookies. Bob led the annual Yard Sale and Clergy Day Celebration. Kay prepared certificates for every minister present at Clergy Day. She also provided resources and leadership at the annual pricing party and yard sale.

Kay's father and mother were very proud of her from the day she was born. She was the oldest child and helped take care of her siblings, Jane, Jim, and Marsha Ann. My mother and father were blessed with the daughter they never had when Kay and I married. She is a blessing to all, my best friend and soul mate, Kay Frances Ward Stegall.

Have Some Turkey and Gravy

Greetings, Chief Eagle Feather. It is splendid that you and your party have welcomed us to this bountiful land of forest. Our feet are a bit unsteady, as we have been at sea for a spell. Looking at the stars is fancy, but our freedom gave us disputes. After a while, it is hard to really be sure we are following the North Star. It is rather controversial to fix our ship to a star that is North when we are not sure if we are going North, South, East, or West. Your greeting is soothing to our spent spirits as we come ashore from the Taurus, LaSabre, and Dakota.

This corn on the cob is awesome. We are weary of fish just now, but next year the maize could be ground, and fish could be breaded for a Thanksgiving meal. There is talk of someone coming here from Spain and bringing fruits or vegetables. We like our native tomatoes. This ground grain would be a good way to batter a sliced green tomato soaked in buttermilk, and fried in buffalo fat to be served as a Thanksgiving appetizer.

The turkey is a wonderful idea. Did you spear it, shoot it with a bow and arrow, or feed from hatch in a willow limb woven cage? However, it is delicious—roasted brown, white meat, and good bone handle grips. I would like to keep some of these feathers. While we will not wear feathers in headbands, it would be fitting to wear a feather on our hats.

We will always treasure your benevolent spirit.
May The Great Spirit bless you throughout the ages,
as we have been blessed with Happy Thanksgiving.
The turkey is fantastic: Chief Eagle Feather, next
year we will bring the gravy.

"Wake up, Bob. It is Thanksgiving" "Oh, good
morning, Kay. Happy Turkey Day!"

The Teacher
Written by Kay Stegall
For a memorial service Dr. Roger Carstensen in the Garden of
Gethsemane
March 30, 1996

Whither shall I go to seek Thy spirit?
Or whither shall I run to find Thy presence?

If I ascend to the Mount of Beatitudes,
remembering holy words spoken to both disciple and
seeker,
you are there.

When I kneel at the foot of Mt. Hermon
and place my fingers into the cool water of the springs
of Banya,
you are there.

When I walk through the splendid black columns
of the synagogue in Capernaum,
you are there.

If I take the wings of the morning and stand on the
shore of the

Galilee, listening to the creaking of the boat, watching the gulls,
drinking in the hillside, in that calm moment,
you are there.

If I walk in the shadow of the olive trees, or see the lush palms;
when I see red anemones, white almond blossoms, fields of yellow mustard blooms,
you are there.

When the stark beauty of the Judean desert fills my eyes,
when the ibex stands on a sheer cliff, undaunted,
you are there.

When I stand on the Mount of Olives,
and look across the valley to the gleaming city of Jerusalem,
a city holding such fear, and such promise,
you are there.

And like so many who have sat at your feet for all too brief a moment, if I look into my heart,
you are there.

Three C's of Success

There are many lessons we learn about threes. As a little boy who made many of my own toys, I learned it is hard to make a stick stand by itself, unless you drive it into the ground. Two sticks can hold each other up until a breeze blows and then they both fall down. Three sticks is the answer, if they lean together at the top of the stand. I learned that in the backyard between marble games.

Christians discover three ways God works, and we lift up the tripod of the trinity. God is creator, so we affirm the heavenly father as divine creator. God sent his son to redeem us from ways we miss the mark, so we affirm Jesus Christ as our redeemer. We all need help to do good and serve God. God blesses our feelings and minds with the leading of the Holy Spirit. We praise God for helping us stand up to our possibilities.

There are three C's toward success—communication, commitment, and consequences. In communication, we use "they" a lot. "Why did "they" do that? What do "they" plan to do?" The second level is commitment that is marked by "we". ""We" are moving ahead. "We" look forward to our next chapter. "We" are a team. The third level is consequences that reflect what God is doing. We had a wonderful worship service, and I felt the presence of the lord. We are getting together with New Vibes. God is good to help our reunion happen. "We are on holy ground." Praise God!

Commitment is a big step forward for each of us. Together we move on to God's purposes. Commitment is full of promise. "Give, and it shall be given you, full, pressed down, shaken together, running over." (Luke 6:38)

What Would Jesus Drive?

While riding in my truck, going to an interim ministry, I was listening to a sports station on the radio. A caller rang the phone and asked, "If Jesus was traveling our roads today, what would he drive?" The question was a response to opposition to SUV vehicles getting low mileage per gallon of gas. After some propositions seasoned with a bit of humor, the phone rang again and another caller answered, "Jesus would ride a Honda because the scripture says, 'they continued daily with one accord.'" The humorous, economic and soulful answer leads us to a deeper truth of our relationship with Christ.

There is no place I feel more "in one accord" than at the Lord's Table. It is an experience as simple as eating our daily bread, and as deep as remembering his sacrificial blood to deliver us from the power of sin and death. It is a Communion. It is an experience of community. I have belonged to many congregations with great diversity, but there is a oneness that is experienced at the Lord's Table that transcends time when we gather as "the body of Christ." Jesus said, "This do in remembrance of me." There are many brothers and sisters with whom I share God's love at the Lord's Table. The relationship is a bridge to past, present, and future. "My cup overflows" when we gather "in one accord". Let us partake with thanksgiving.

Kinks in the Hose

When we built our house, Greenbo, 10 years ago, we wanted a water supply for every inch of space, in both the house and the yard. The water comes from Spring Park, where the Indians and Settlers lived because of the spring flowing 24/7/365 days a year. We added two purification systems to make sure the water was pure and the iced tea was clear. It works.

Our builder installed five water faucets in the yard, two in the front and three in the back. They are very special faucets; Simmons faucets, standing three feet, with a lockable level control on the top. They drain themselves automatically, so we do not worry about them when it freezes in the winter. The water pressure is actually stronger in the yard faucets than in the smaller outlets in the house.

We water the flowers, corn, tomatoes, pecan trees, dogwood trees, yellow jacket nests, St. Augustine grass, fire ant hill, sunflower plants, Bermuda grass, shrubs, etc. The key to reaching everything is the hose. We put three fifty-foot hoses together and move it around as the work demands. The hose will always get a kink and the water flow stops. The more we move around, the more kinks we will get. What is a water hose without water? What is work without some kinks?

Undoing kinks is a part of the work. There are three ways to unkink a hose—swirl it, shake it, or change directions. One of them always works. Seldom do we work to bring the blessings of water to the thirsty plants that we do not have a kink in the hose.

When the water stops flowing, we come to attention. There is so much to share, so many thirsty needs. Swirl, shake, change directions. Praise the Lord! The water flows abundantly. It is a blessing to learn from kinks in the hose.

Oh, you poor thirsty, wilted plant. We can reach you. "Come on hose."

Wish We Were There
by Kay Stegall

Somewhere the sky is blue
    The sun is warm
The waves are rolling
    Full of charm.

Wish we were there.

When summer comes
    Throughout the land
It is time to dig
    Your toes in the sand.

Wish we were there.

So in July, let's
    Find a place
Where for a week we can
    Tan our face
Get some sun
    And have some fun.

Let's take a vacation
    We will make the reservation.

Wish we were there.

Family conference
    Required to set the date
Papa and Mimi will pay the rate!

Wish we were there.

Little Foxes That Spoil the Vineyard

Sometimes I saw foxes when I was hunting on the farm. Daddy blamed the noises in the hen house at night on little foxes. One day after school, a red tailed fox crossed the street from the High School to the Kudzu covered bank on the other side. Recently, one evening at dusk, I saw three foxes eating table scraps I had dumped near the sand pile at Greenbo. You never know where you will see a little fox. It could be woods, fields, backyard, school, or street. The game officers said we should not feed little foxes as it made them dependent on our generosity. They may also carry rabies. Even King Solomon cautioned about "the little foxes that spoil the vineyard" (Song of Solomon 2:15)

I officiated at a wedding a few weeks ago at the Robert Trent Jones Golf Trail Club on the banks of the Tennessee River. The groom is a friend. He talked about his wedding for months: right time, place, weather, honeymoon, guests, etc. A week before his long planned wedding he called me and said, "My preacher will be out of town on our wedding date. Will you do the ceremony?" I said, "For my friend, I will be glad to help." It was lovely. Even the golfers stopped their carts and watched the glamour and listened to the beautiful harp music. After the ceremony, the photographer was making pictures. A little fox came over the hill, stretched out on the ground, watched, listened, and began rolling in the grass. He became the center of attention. I am glad he waited for his performance until after the bride and groom said, "I do." His innocence was captivating, but his timing was a bit off. I hope someone took his picture. He was beautiful. His red tail matched the groom's bright vest. Maybe he was "a sign". Where is the cake and punch?

ROAD SPILL

There was a dead rabbit lying in the yard. That brings up the question of how it got there. Maybe it was the neighbor's dogs that came for their daily visit and grabbed the startled rabbit when it ran out from under the brush pile. The rabbit was probably waiting for the grandkids to come for their Bird Tribe Rain Dance. Maybe the rabbit committed rabbitcide because we had ten inches of snow and Mother Nature's food supply was frozen in winter wonder land. The rabbit's head and two front legs were missing. Some critter must have ambushed it and run away when the buzzard got too close for comfort. There is always the question of why? Who? What? How? It is human nature to ask questions about how Mother Nature works.

A seven hour drive to Orange Beach can be a seven hour class on wit and wisdom loaded with questions about road kill. Why are those purple splashes on the road? It could have been a wreck and the state troopers marked the spots for insurance companies in contest for the right, the wrong, and the claims for damages. But the pattern of the dried paint told me someone did not tie down and seal all they were hauling on their trailer. A can of paint fell to the road and left its mark, leaving a visible lesson to secure what you haul, big or small. I saluted a state trooper whose blue lights were flashing behind a pickup truck. The truck had been pulling a trailer loaded with planks, boards, and pipes hanging over the rear with no red flags to warn the texting, cell phoning , snacking, tail gating, bullet driver who was chasing the vision of being on time.

What was that on the bridge? It was as flat as a flitter. Cars and trucks ran over it so many times it took the form of a pancake. The bridge was long and had high sides. The dead animal became a victim of its choice. A deer needs to get to the other side of the road. Its buddies may have already crossed. It was detained by a few more bites of acorns. Yes, it can catch up because it is fast on the hooves. The eighteen wheeler was faster and trying to dodge at the last minute causing the deer to turn onto the bridge. There was no escape from the fast traffic. A little extra time could have made a difference. Procrastination can hurt man and beast.

Watching for the crows on the road is a way of seeing road kill. My crow buddies, Frank, Jessie, and Friend always appear wherever I go. When I grew up on the farm, I thought crows only ate corn. They came to the barn to eat with the mules and hogs. They came to the fields where we had planted the corn crop and they came back when we harvested the corn. But, traveling over the years taught me that crows love to eat road kill. They hover over a crushed rabbit, gather around a smashed dog, and peck on an unlucky coyote. To estimate distance we may say, "As the crow flies." But wisdom can come to one who watches where the crow pecks. Observing road kill is a lesson in caution: Better to be safe than sorry.

It is amazing how much litter we see along the roads today. It is not dead animals but trash that people have thrown out of their cars and trucks to keep their vehicles clean. Are you finished with that burger? Don't put that dirty tissue on the seat. Give it to me and I will throw it out the window. I just hate these plastic bags. Toss it out the window. Look at the old cotton field. Looks like it is growing a crop of plastic bags. Sometimes trash is not what I throw out the window but the one who throws it, spoiling God's beautiful world. Crows can be a sign of our wayward times when we travel. Did you see those crows pecking inside that bag? They found someone's discarded chicken lunch! We have moved to another era, ROAD SPILL. How and what we discard says a lot about us. Watch and listen to the crows.

Chapter 11
To Be A Millionaire

To Be a Millionaire

Serving seven churches over 50 years of ministry was an opportunity to become a millionaire. The student churches were at Newbern and Crab Orchard, Tennessee in 1956-57. Full time ministries in Tennessee were at Bells, Springfield, and Macon Christian Church in Memphis. We were 18 years at First Christian Church, Florence, Alabama before moving to First Christian Church in Little Rock, Arkansas. Kay and I are finishing our 11th interim ministry after serving churches in Birmingham, Athens, Hartselle, Cedar Plains, Decatur, Valhermoso Springs, Florence, Huntsville, and Madison. The people we met, ministries, and learning experiences are what money cannot buy.

Marrying my high school sweetheart at Humboldt, Tennessee has been a rich heritage of old and new memories. Kay grew up in town, and her family worked at the bank. I grew up on the farm, and worked in the fields. We both went to church on Sundays with our families. We knew who taught school, ran the movie theatre, cooked the best hamburgers in town, policed the streets, belonged to the civic clubs, and had floats in the Strawberry Festival Parade. From day one, we could talk the talk while we walked the walk. On Thanksgiving, we took our three children, Pat, Maryjane, and Jennifer back home to be with both of our families, all in one day. Some things we can never find on Wall Street.

I wonder how many breaths I breathe in a day? If I multiply that by 365, and multiply that by over 70 years, then I am a millionaire. Praise the Lord! What a happy Thanksgiving! I take a deep breath, exhale, and thank God. I count these riches every day. God is good!

I'll Think About That

Billy was my older brother by 22 months. When we walked home from school or rode our bicycles he was always ahead of me. On the hill on Highway 45 I would slow down and holler, "wait up Billy." He slowed, waited a little and went on down the road. Whether going to school or home from school, Billy always had a goal, a plan, and was thinking about how to get there. In conversations or suggestions he often replied, without saying yes or no, "I'll think about that."

Since he was the older brother I could always blame my shortcomings on Billy. We were asked why we went down Sugar Creek. Why did we leave our clothes under the bridge when we ran in the sand to the Forked Deer River? Why did we walk down the railroad to the river without shoes and tie paper plates to our feet while we walked on the hot rails, gravel and creosoted crossties? Trying not to fault myself, I usually said, "Billy told me." It wasn't long until I was not taken seriously. If Bobby said it, ask Billy.

He was always my good example. Daddy bought a single row tractor and Billy became the primary driver. He was the driver and power lift, raising and lowering the plows with a hand-operated lever. A few years later Daddy purchased a new two-row tractor. Billy knew how to drive and operated it the first day. He was gifted in figuring out machinery. The first trailer was the frame of an old Pontiac car. We hauled cabbage to the crossing for the market. Billy could back that trailer to sit on a dime. He was an expert. When I purchased our fishing boat a few years ago, I practiced catching up with him by backing the boat trailer into our one stall garage. I did bump the wall a few times.

The bridge over Sugar Creek to the back forty acres was built of tree logs and planks put together by family and friends. The floods often moved the bridge or washed it down the creek. We expected to replace the bridge every few years. Mother Nature usually presented the challenge. The last time it was replaced, I joined Daddy and Billy on the project. We dug holes for the tree posts, moving up a notch by sinking metal barrels in the sand, sinking the posts and filling in around them with concrete. Billy was the primary engineer. He stopped, backed up on the bank, and studied the big picture. Wanting to not waste conversation time, I talked. Daddy said, "Son, come sit on the log with me. We will talk. Billy is thinking."

After serving in the military, Billy returned to the farm. He and his wife, Jo Ann, bought the Adam's farm. Their children Ricky, Betty Ann and John grew up on the farm. They purchased more land that joined their property. They all worked hard and fulfilled a life long dream of owning land from Highway 45 to the railroad. Billy looked at the big picture, focused, looked down the road, managed money well and earned the respect of bankers, neighbors, family, friends, churches and community.

A few years ago, Mr. Raines, Vocational Agriculture Teacher, called and invited Kay and me back to Humboldt for their Annual Banquet. In High School, Billy had served as an officer in the FFA (Future Farmers of America). He was asked by his teacher,

Mr. Shankle, and his principal, Mr. Wilson, to drive our truck to Nashville so they could shop for the school at the Surplus Store.

When he called, Mr. Raines said, "Bobby, we are honoring your brother, Billy, as Farmer of the Year. He has supported our Farm Training Projects by harvesting the crops with his big John Deere equipment. He never charged us a penny. We want to express our appreciation for his generous spirit." I didn't even have to think about that. I said, "Thomas, you know that Kay and I will be there. Thank you for this special recognition of Billy."

One day a few years later, I went home and Billy was driving the tractor in the field next to Highway 45. I stopped at the store and bought him some snacks. That was a family tradition. If you stopped by the country store bring some snacks for the people working in the field. He was delighted and together we ate everything in the paper sack. He had an errand to run and asked me if I wanted to drive the tractor a little while. It was a big John Deere so he had to show me how to start, go, stop, and adjust the speed. I enjoyed learning the modern way of farming. It was a hot day in July and I was scorching in the sunshine. I remembered what you could do with a paper sack. Using the sack that I'd brought snacks into the field, I folded and placed it on my head. It blocked the sun. What a relief! Around home, people always gave the raised hand greeting when passing. Several people honked the horn and waved at me. Billy passed by in his truck on the way to town to run his errand. But he soon returned. and walked out into the field. I stopped and he handed me a cap. He said, "Bobby, put this cap on your head. When people pass by, they think that's me wearing that paper sack." How thoughtful. It made us both laugh, especially Billy. It gave us both a smile that was for time and eternity.

When I go back home to Humboldt I walk among friends who knew and loved my big brother, William Clark Stegall, Jr. When they mention Billy, I feel right at home.

Two White Ribbons

Serving in eleven interim ministries over twelve years requires a lot of traveling. Five different cars were purchased and used for this purpose. They were all used cars, but perfect for the commuting. There was a Taurus, a Sable, and three LeSabres. We covered a lot of roads, highways, and interstates. We learned to identify places, people, and activities in the repetitive trips. The longest interim was over seventeen months. The shortest was six months.

One person who became very special to us was Roy Lee. He lived in a little block house painted white. It had a green roof, small front and back porches, little windows, and a chimney. A small air conditioner was in one window. At night, there was barely any light in the house, just a small glow in a front room, like reflections from a television. On some days, clothes were hanging on a clothesline in the backyard.

During the week, we might see Roy Lee walking up the road with a fishing pole to a roadside slough. Sometimes he carried a plastic gallon jug of water back home from a neighbor's house. We always looked forward to waving at Roy Lee on Sunday mornings. He sat on the front porch, even in chilly weather, reading his Bible at 8 o'clock in the morning. Yes, he was going to church. Later in the day, he was walking back home, dressed in a suit and carrying his Bible. Somehow he always knew it was the Lord's Day.

    One day, I stopped to meet Roy Lee. I brought him some diet drinks, and he said he appreciated them because diabetes was a health issue for him. At Christmas, I dropped off some warm blankets. He said, "Thank you very much." My fishing season was good, so I took him several bags of frozen fish. He put them in an old freezer on the back porch, and said his sister loved fried catfish. He knew he was going to a fish fry at her house.

    Last week, there were two white ribbons on the porch posts above the stone steps. What does this mean, we pondered. That night, there was no dim light in the front room. The shades were gone from the windows, and the house was empty. In the pasture next to the house, there were hundreds of white seagulls gathered on a little hill. Even mother nature was bringing another tribute to Roy Lee. We miss him so much at his house, but we will always see him in our minds. There he is, Bible in hand, shaking hands with people by the pearly gates. Our destiny is really God's House. Jesus said, "In my father's house are many rooms." Two white ribbons honor the past, and beckon the future.

We Got Mail

Mr. Waddell sent us a letter saying our offer on the lot for building Greenbo, our new home, had been accepted. We moved into the house in late October of '97. We planted some trees, and saved one special tree that was getting a good start in the old horse pasture. Mr. Waddell said we could have one horse for each acre. I said, "Well, that means we can have a horse and a half." He nodded and laughed.

The tree we saved was named Osage Orange by the Native Americans. The wood was strong and bendable, so it was a popular resource for making bows and arrows. I have made bows and arrows from the time I could walk to the cane thicket. I sure wanted that tree to stay in our yard. The tree has thorns, grapefruit size fruit that some call horse apples, and lots of shade.

A part of our inheritance is under that tree. Kay's lovely aunt, Nana, who was a saint to us, sat in a metal swing in the yard. I can see her now swinging in the cool of the evening. When she died, they asked me if there was anything I wanted from Nana's house, and I said, "Her swing." I shaped that tree like an umbrella, and the swing is there under the shade, inviting me to a feast of precious memories. Watching birds at the feeder, and sitting in that swing under that tree can be called my "Prayer Time" as I get close to The Great Spirit.

This week, one horse apple fell to the ground. I looked for more, but zero. I searched the tree, and no horse apples. Usually, I pick up horse apples for weeks in a five gallon can, and take them to the forest. What! Just one horse apple this year? Oh, the late freeze. Sure, that is what it is... Oh well, I don't have a horse, and I do have a bow and arrow. I'll get back to my inheritance, "Just a Swangin'." In the shade.

The Horror Cope

The words of our president yesterday that made headlines were "Ignore Wall Street". The reason is the DOW has fallen in six months by one half its value, to less than 7,000. There is a mood of panic in the air, and people are pondering about what may be next. One guy on the news said with a bit of humor waged against the horror, "If your neighbor loses their job, that is a recession. If you lose your job, that is a depression." There is a mood of depression in the air, taxing spent spirits for spending spirits.

Our heating and air-conditioning company called us about replacing the unit in our 12 year old house. He explained the unit usually lasted 10 to 15 years, and a good deal on a new unit would be a good move. He said improving home efficiency was a part of the stimulus package. We could get a $1,500 tax credit next year. We took the deal, and the workers came on a cold winter day. Mid morning, we wanted to serve them cups of hot chocolate. I went to a dollar store to buy cups. They cost one dollar for twenty. It was $1.09 with tax. She asked, "Would you like to donate to the children's reading program?" I gave her the $.91 change for the donations jar. Well, that cost $2.00. Even a helping hand needs something in it.

There are three things I usually read on the comic page of the local paper: Wizard of Id, Hagar the Horrible, and my Horoscope. Every day is a learning experience. My Horoscope said: "Jot down a few notes about being frugal to include in the book you are writing. List all the things a person should not do—like, don't go grocery shopping while you are hungry." This is scary. How did my horoscope know I was writing a book? Hagar the Horrible was talking French toast with the French army because he could not speak French. The Wizard of Id observed a generous king giving away shirts off other people's backs.

Well, here are seven things I learned about being frugal. I learned it on the family farm, in community, higher education, being a minister, banks, books, friends, etc.

1. If you don't plant in the spring, you cannot expect to harvest in the fall.
2. There is a chicken hawk always trying to get your chickens, little and big.
3. Eat when you are hungry, but don't waste your money because you have it.
4. Don't put all your eggs in one basket, diversify your potential.
5. Make friends with bankers, and prove your character in performance.
6. Share something with others so that they can count their blessings.
7. Accept gifts from others with a "thank you", and they can have the joy of sharing.

It would be nice to have a "Managing Your Money" party and write a Proverbs 32 chapter. Let's see. A penny saved is a penny earned. Take care of the dimes, and the dollars will take care of themselves. You can always borrow more than you can pay back. Don't even try to keep up with the Jones. Buy a big "Ben Hur" deep freeze, and lay by in store. Plant a garden and save yourself a trip to the grocery store. Buy what you need, and use what you buy.

If we Horror Cope every day, then we are on our way to better times. I may not read my Horoscope every day in the newspaper, but I will cope: borrow from Peter to pay Paul, shift that to the other account, let the refund take care of that, a potted meat sandwich for lunch, hello friends-it is good to see you on Main Street, turn off the TV news, skip the front page on the newspaper and read the Comic page. Sometimes, wisdom is where you least expect to find it. It is wiser to horror cope before the spook scares us. Happy trails to you...Yes, Mr. President, "I will ignore Wall Street." My best friends are on Main Street.

The Little House

Odell and Margie lived in a little house. The Wallers built it when the government took over their farm at Milan to develop the arsenal for winning World War 11. It was not painted like their new house. It was the farm house for the share croppers to work a few acres of row crops. The two mules had a shed for shelter during rain or cold weather. The little house was built under beautiful tall trees on a hill overlooking highway 45. The Saturday Night Dance Hall was a stone's throw up the road toward town. Sometimes, Odell and Margie turned off the radio and just listened to the music next door. I never saw them without a smile on their faces.

Walter and Millie were share croppers. They lived in three different unpainted houses in our neighborhood. The family was big and growing. Walter came to our back door one evening and said, "Mr. Clark, Millie has tuck down on me. I need some baking soda to give her for relief." A few hours later, my brother, Bill, drove her to the hospital where she gave birth to another baby. I played cowboys with one of their sons. He had a pistol holster, made from an old leather shoe. I so admired it, he gave it to me when I went home. I guess he had another old shoe. His gift became my treasure. Walter and Millie lived on the hill above Little Sugar Creek. I could walk up the creek to their house in the field. I don't remember a road. They never had a car. But, they had a lot of molasses and corn bread.

    I thought of my friends and neighbors yesterday at lunch. I was Kay's chauffeur for one of her trips to the Regional Office, where she serves as Moderator Elect of the Christian Church (Disciples of Christ) in Alabama-Northwest Florida. Before she went into her meeting, sweet Kay gave me a twenty dollar bill to buy a loaf of bread at Edgar's, and a treat for my lunch. At noon I arrived at my favorite restaurant. I requested a seat by the window. I ordered—unsweetened tea with lemon, and a country dinner of fried chicken livers, breaded okra, stewed apples, and cornbread. It was a feast. The only part missing was my soul mate and best friend, Kay. To top off my meal, I requested some warm syrup to pour on my cornbread. I didn't think they would have molasses. I left with a sense of fullness and well-being. I thought of my friends in little houses, who had big hearts and full bellies.

    One day when I was attending High School, Daddy said, "We are going to move back to our little house."

When Papa died and Granny Stegall moved in with Aunt Buddy and Potts, we moved to the big house next to Highway 45. I loved to sit in the swing, eat apples and ripe tomatoes, and watch the traffic. Daddy had a budget. He went to the bank and borrowed $5,000 to build. We tore away all of the little house except the living room and one bedroom. We added the kitchen, back porch, a bedroom, a formal living room, plus a nice front porch. Daddy, and friends: Dalton, Ernest, and Charles, and Billy and I built the house—in budget. The little house became the bigger house.

The house is there today. The room where I was born, where grandchildren gathered, and neighbors played Rook still stands. We are adding central heating and air this month. Sometimes houses are too little. Sometimes they are too big. Sometimes houses are just right. Love makes a big difference.

Depositing Affirmations

Saturday mornings in Crockett County were special joys in the late 50's. The radio featured a very special music couple. They sang a duet while he played the guitar. After each song, they advertised their sponsor.

"Get your car washed... at the "Whiz Car Wash"... on the corner of 5th and Main... downtown... across from the Baptist Church... a fourth of July special... one half price on a special day... you can't beat that deal..."

"Ain't that right, Little Virginia Sweetheart?" "That's right, Cowboy Lee!" "Well, let's sing another song, "Get up and get goin' ". "That strikes a cord for me, Darlin'." "Next we will do "Davy, Davy Crockett, King of the Wild Frontier". "Sounds good to me, honey."

Another deposit of affirmations came by the good example of our neighbors, Monroe and Icy. They didn't own a car, but lived close to the city limits. Saturday afternoon was the day to heat the bath water in a wash pot with a fire in the backyard. The water went in a tin tub, and was tempered with cool well water. After the bath, it was dress up time for going to town. They walked down to the side of Highway 45 and looked for some good person to stop and give them a ride. Mr. Williams, another neighbor, said he stopped and invited them aboard. He heard Monroe say, "Miss Icy, you look good to me." She replied with a smile, "Thank you, Monroe, you do, too." Off to town they go. Have a good time. Come home and be happy. One went to the Pool Room. One went to the Black and White Clothing Store. Both went to U-Totem's Grocery. And back home he said, "I will open the door for you, Darlin'." She said, "Thank you, Honey Pot."

Depositing affirmations is a good investment, but one must be wise that a swindle may be in the air. On the way to a favorite fishing hole, I stopped for a bucket of minnows. The nice young lady came out of the store about daylight, and put a half pound of minnows in the bucket. I had paid inside, but gave her a dollar tip. She said, "Thank you, honey." I stopped by the truck stop to get bags of ice. The lady said, "With tax that will be three dollars and twenty four cents." She gave me change from the five dollar bill and said, "Have a nice day, sweetie." At the breakfast house, I ordered bacon, eggs, pancakes and syrup to go along with my coffee. When the lady brought my order and placed it on the table she said, "Hope you enjoy, honey."

What a blessing to live down south. People do the honey talk. It is hard to have a bad day when so many deposits of affirmations come your way, from daylight to dark, and past the evening news. "Good night, darlin'." "Hope you sleep good, sweetie." What a wealth of riches when people generously give the deposit of their affirmations, with no strings attached. We have been spoiled by the Grand Ole Opry... but I love it, Darlin'.

As the Crow Flies

Someone will ask, "Where do you live?" I answer, "At Tuscumbia, Alabama. It is the birthplace of Helen Keller, the Lady of Courage". Then we talk about what it is near to get a sense of direction, especially if they are coming to our house for a fish fry. It is about a mile from the Alabama Hall of Fame. Seeing some puzzle on the face, I add an escape route by saying, "about a mile as the crow flies". After we affirmed the route by air, then we start talking about signs, roads, turns, etc.

We could just say, "Go to the Alabama Hall of Fame on Highway 72 to Corinth and follow the crows. The crows always show up at our house. They were on the farm in Tennessee. When we lived in Florence, three crows came to the backyard every day looking for leftovers in the grass pile. I named them: Frank, Jessie, and Friend. They liked us. We moved to Little Rock, and they came to my garden in the backyard by our Little Sugar Creek. That was a 250 mile trip, so I respectfully started saluting Frank, Jessie, and Friend every morning.

At Greenbo, we have added three bird feeders and three bird baths. Guess who comes to see us everyday. Yes, Frank, Jessie, and Friend. I continue my tradition of saluting. It is a way I identify myself and honor them. It is something I do everyday when I hear the "caw, caw, caw". In fact, I don't feel like I am having a good day until my friends show up and I give them a salute. An observant neighbor questioned my loyalty one day, and I passed it off as quickly as I could with "better to salute a crow than eat one." That gave us both something to chew on. He left to go hunt turkeys. I smiled and went fishing.

A Fairy Ring

Keeping an eye on a neighbor's house while they are on vacation can bring a blessing. They left us the key, and asked us to get their mail. Naturally, we kept an eye on the yard, too. It was in the yard where we saw the fairy ring grow rounder each day. It began with half a dozen mushrooms, bleached white, six inches tall, and round as a saucer at the top. They came up in a semi-circle. Each day another six or eight came up until a complete circle was formed. Kay saw it from the kitchen window one morning and said, "Oh, look! There is a fairy ring." It was in perfect view on the gentle hill slope.

When our daughter and grandchildren came for a visit late one evening Kay said, "Caroline and Kevin, let's go see the fairy ring." They ran with excitement and anticipation of a drama, and we followed. "Mimi, what is a fairy ring?" Kay was a ballet dancer when she was a little girl; so, so knew how to explain to the imagination. She said, "When a fairy ring grows, fairies will come in the night and dance in the ring. The moon is full, and when the fairies come, they will dance with splendor." It was not a burning bush. The ring was just mushrooms, up for a few days and nights, then, gone forever. Will the fairies make it on time?

Mimi said, "Oh look! There is Twinkle Toes." Twinkle Toes was a baby rabbit that Caroline, Kevin, and Maryjane brought from school in the spring. Some children were harassing it, and the mother was not to be found. They had let it go into one of Papa's brush piles near the forest back of the yard. They always asked, "Do you think Twinkle Toes is OK?" They were so excited to see Twinkle Toes, fully grown and eating grass. They stepped out of the fairy ring, and sneaked quietly across the yard to get closer to Twinkle Toes. He looked, paused, and ran into the forest. They laughed with joy and jumped with glee. The fairy ring brought five fairies and a rabbit. This is a better memory than mushroom soup. It is soul food.

There's a Snake

    The Bible lays out the facts of life in the Garden of Eden when Genesis 3 says, "Now the serpent was more crafty than any other wild animal the Lord had made." One never knows when you may see a snake. Life is a mixture of good and bad, so we have a reminder to be on our watch and make good choices. A snake can be as innocent as a little green snake, or as hurtful as a copperhead or cottonmouth moccasin. Growing up on Sugar Creek produced a lot of snake stories. Some stories bring laughter and some bring tears. That is just the way it is with a snake.

    X.L. and Brooksie were sharecroppers on our farm. The house was provided, as well as land, tools, mules, and resources. After the crops were sold, the expenses were paid, and money shared as agreed with the sharecropper and land owner. It was a benefit for both, and provided a way to exist in a world where money did not flow from the government to help people without jobs. X.L. and Brooksie had four sons, two about my age and two younger boys. We were friends with the Barnetts, and cherish some happy times. X.L. was really afraid of snakes.

    Daddy always found time to take us crappie fishing in April and May. We would take two days and a night to travel to Lick Creek, and fish. Daddy bought a small boat—aluminum, no motor, barely room for two. He and X.L. were fishing with cane poles and minnows. Daddy sat in the front of the boat and moved the paddle, twisting it and pulling with it in the water. We called that "sculling". He and X.L. were fishing under the willows at the bank, and Daddy was ready to move to another place. He "sculled" but the boat never moved. He turned to X.L. and said, "We are not moving." X.L. said, "No, I am holding this willow branch till that snake passes." Daddy looked up and saw the snake swimming to the other bank. X.L. was truly afraid of snakes. We still laugh about that paralyzed boat.

X.L came in from the field one day at noon for lunch, and Brooksie was on the front porch screaming and crying. He ran to her to help and she said, "There is a snake on our feather bed." X.L. went to the back door, went in the house, and got his shotgun. He came back, stood on the porch, and shot through the screen door to kill the snake. The snake died on the spot, and so did the feather bed. We laughed at how the feathers flew all over the house. Bam! There they went, like a chicken that got hit by a truck on the highway.

One day, we were picking tomatoes for market. The field was about one acre along the banks of Sugar Creek. We harvested the staked tomatoes by picking the big green ones and pinkies. We were picking four rows, and Red, our mule, pulled a wooden sled between the rows with seven bushel boxes on top. We emptied the buckets of tomatoes in the boxes. All seven were full. Daddy took the sled to the shade tree to unload the seven boxes and get empty ones for the next filling. We sat on the road bank, waiting, drinking water, talking, teasing, and resting. X.L. sat on a bucket. Some of us had thrown our buckets up on the road bank into the johnson grass. One broke loose and rolled toward X.L. He jumped up and ran out into the field fifty feet before he stopped and looked back. Yes, he thought it was a snake. Instead, it was a good laugh. He thought, "There's a snake." Real or imagined, it is still scary. Thank God for the laughs along the way.

May I Be Excused?

    Miss Watson asked me one day if our third grade class could make a walking trip out to the family farm. I asked Mother and Daddy, and they said, "Yes." It was about three miles from the elementary school, just past Little Sugar Creek that ran in front of the house. It was a long walk, and everyone brought a sack lunch. We didn't have a herd of cows to observe, and the mules were in the field pulling plows. No one really wanted to look at pigs. They just wanted to eat a bologna sandwich under the catalpa tree.

    Naturally, we heard, "I need to be excused." It was a polite request for a restroom break. Well, you have two choices. You can go to the barn and use corn cobs and shucks, or you can go to the little toilet house out in the back yard. It was a one stall unpainted shack that sat over a square grave-like hole that could be gradually topped with fresh dirt. It was our best "modern convenience" available at the time. The blessings of last Christmas were still available because we saved the fresh white and soft wrapping paper in a bushel basket in our "outhouse". The Christmas Eve family gift opening at Papa and Granny's kept us supplied for quite a while. In the fall when the white tissue paper supply ran out, an old Sears catalog with soft yellow advertising pages became the order of the day. Yesterday's stimulus package is a long way from today's.

    Most farm houses had little shacks out back, progress from the alternative of going to the woods. What is natural has always found its way in the realm of mother nature. Where could our country be without Indians and cowboys? Who would form a mule train to go out west and settle land if they had a criteria to meet that was beyond their financial landscape? There is a difference in getting spoiled and getting back to basics. In fact, once we forget the basics, the spoiling spills over into a stink that is worse than thoughtless, like neighbors burning wet leaves on a windless day. The smell just won't go away.

Last month, we returned to our home church for a visit. My third grade teacher had gone to church there sixty four years ago. I remember where she sat. She was one of my favorite teachers. On our visit back, we sat on the church pew near the aisle where we sat with mother in the later years on the visits back home. Friends came up and greeted us. It was good times again. Loving friends and precious memories over the years. A man about my age, and his wife, took a seat on the other end of the pew. We looked at each other and nodded a friendly greeting. After the service he came up to me and said, "Bob, do you remember me? I am Lloyd. I remember when our third grade class walked out to your farm one day." I said, "Hi, Lloyd. I remember. May I be excused?"

A New Cowboy Comes To Town

Saturday was Cowboy Day for me on the farm. I made a stick horse out of the handle of an old broom. After tying a shoestring on the knob I rode like a streak of lightening. My friend sometimes bragged that he sold his stick horses for a quarter because they were faster than his friends' stick horses. I never sold one of mine but I gently laid it to rest in the shed after Daddy bought Billy and me a pony. His name was Jerry, named after my new cousin, Jerry Thompson. I loved to saddle Jerry and ride to Sugar Creek. One day I learned an important lesson when I was in a hurry to saddle up and ride. Jerry broke into a run and the saddle slid under his belly. I saw a pony from the bottom side up. It was the first and last time I ever saw a pony's belly button.

My cousin, Herman Ray, and I met at Granny and Granddaddy Patterson's house to go to the Saturday Movies at the Ritz or Plaza theatres in Humboldt. Our favorite movies were Gene Autry, Roy Rogers or the Lone Ranger. After the movies we were fired up and could hardly wait to get our cap pistols and run in the yard. We enjoyed acting out the parts in the movie where good cowboys brought justice and compassion, making right the wrongs that bad cowboys inflicted on others. Good cowboys can run fast or be gentle riders. They can sing happy songs and smile at pretty girls. There are ranges and ranches down the trails. Singing always makes the beans taste better at the campfires.

While we lived in Little Rock, our daughter and her family lived in El Paso, where her husband served in the Army. Jennifer and Wellington invited Kay and me to meet them and our grandsons, Justin and Chris, in Phoenix. They had rented an RV, and we camped in the Grand Canyon National Park. One day we went horseback riding. Chris was small and his Dad stayed with him at the barn until we returned.

A couple of years later Jennifer's family visited us in Little Rock. Kay and I had enlarged our deck, planning for family and friends visits. We planted trees, flowers and bushes on our sloping back yard. We added stone steps from the deck to the little garden beside the little creek that I named "Little Sugar Creek." Chris came out-- Cowboy style. He wore a cowboy hat, long gloves and carried a big pistol. He was jumping and running, ready to go and chase the bad guys. We all laughed with hopes and dreams, smiles and sparkling eyes. A new Cowboy comes to town. Happy Trails!

"Here, Bob, Here"

There were many dogs on the farm over the years, but the last dog, Bob, was the king. Dogs were part of the family culture. Some of the earliest pictures of Billy and Bobby were holding puppies. It seemed Daddy was using us to take pictures of the dogs. He just laughed at the idea.

Queen was the first dog I remember. She was a rabbit dog. She was brown and black with long ears. She was tall, and loved attention. She was a good mother, and loved a good brood. She disappeared, mysteriously, and Daddy went to a fortune teller to get some clues. The fortune teller told him Queen was alive and chained in a backyard next to a creek. Daddy never found Queen, but was relieved to know she was still alive.

Scooter was my bird dog. My brother and I got two bird dogs from Mr. Smith, a pharmacist at the drug store. Ben Smith was in Billy's graduating class. He rode his motor bike out to our house to play in the creek with us. The motor bike was used for prescription delivery, and Ben could ride it on

Sundays. I think the connection with Ben helped us get the bird dogs. Mr. Smith hunted quail on our farm, and that didn't hurt either.

I loved quail hunting with Scooter. One day, we found seven coveys of quail. We flushed a covey on the Byrd Place and one lit in a tree. I never imagined a quail would light in a tree. I shot him with my 12 gauge single barrel shotgun. All the other quail I shot were on the flush. I still feel a little bad about shooting a quail sitting in a tree. But when I remember how good they tasted when mother fried quail, I feel better. That day, I bagged five quail and almost got the limit of six. If you don't like to walk, don't take up quail hunting. You usually cover seven farms on one hunt, averaging a covey a farm.

Rabbit hunting is another story. You may stay on one creek all day. I hunted between Sugar Creek and Little Sugar Creek. We had a pack of Beagle hounds. We just called them "rabbit dogs", and handed out names as appropriate. Roy was a sharecropper on the farm, and I loved to hunt with Roy. He never tired of rabbit hunting, and you didn't need a chicken house or hog pen to keep meat on the table. Fried and barbecued rabbit made a house smell good in the winter, and there was no rush from the supper table to listen to Amos and Andy on the radio.

Another thing I enjoyed about rabbit hunting was that you stood in one place for a long time after the dogs jumped the rabbit. The strategy was to let the dogs run the rabbit. A rabbit will eventually circle back to the place they jumped him. Find a high place and watch. While you watch, snack on food in your hunting coat pockets. Oranges and apples from the Christmas tree were good. They were juicy, and comforted your thirst.

As I said earlier, the last dog, Bob, was the king. Bob's mother was an Alaskan Husky. She just showed up one day in the backyard. She wore a collar with a name tag. A phone call was made to the owner. The owner said, "Just keep her if you want her. She is a traveling dog, and she would just leave again if we came to get her." She was fed, and she stayed.

In a few days it was obvious she was soon to be a mother. A wire fence was circled in the tractor shed, and hay was scattered on the ground. She had four beautiful puppies. They had long hair, and favored a German Shepherd. Their daddy would have been proud. They stayed behind the fence until it became overcrowded, and Mom and her pups were set free. When the pups were at the weaning age, mother walked off toward the Highway 45 bridge over Sugar Creek. One little male struggled, deciding whether to stay or go. He went for a little while, and turned back to the place of his birth. It was a sad goodbye to his mother and siblings, but the tears would anoint him King.

Granny named him "Bob". Bob was her father's name, Bob Patterson. Really, it was Robert Austin Patterson, but everyone called him Bob. Granny talked to King Bob. She fed him scraps from the table, and on occasion, the best of the "vittles". Granny loved to cook and share. Bob never went hungry at Granny's door. She bought hamburger on sale at Big Star, and stored hamburger balls in the freezer. Bob came to the back door every morning and stood. Granny came to the door and rolled out a hamburger ball to him with the good morning greeting, "Here, Bob". He took the cold prize, walked a few feet, lay down, and had a king's feast.

Bob developed a strong personality. It probably was the farm setting with sixty brood sows, pastures of little pigs, and flocks of black birds feasting on the goodies. He barked, ran, gave orders and commands. He was King Bob. He had some competition from three other dogs that just showed up. A big collie had a bowel problem and carried a little "leave overs" on his back legs. Trip had lost a back leg and hopped around like he never needed four legs. Pee Wee just looked for a place to fit in, for it seemed a dog was everywhere he wanted to go. But, they all knew the pecking order, and Bob was first. In time, he was the first... and last.

Things were never the same after Granny died. Bob missed her, too. Their daily ritual disappeared. No more hamburger balls in the morning, or sitting at her feet when she was sitting in the backyard swing. He took up with nephew John, and slept in brother Bill's garage. When I hauled limbs from tree trimming at Greenbo in Alabama back to the farm, Bob followed the truck to the creek. He was slow, staggered some, but always followed me to the creek. I pitched him snacks of crackers, fries, and cookies. And sometimes I lightly tickled him between the ears. He always led the way up the road back to the house after I unloaded the limbs. He took his time, and I followed the king.

The first year after Mother died, we worked in the flowerbeds, trying to make them maintenance free. We also upgraded the vacant house to be safe and secure. I was born in that house. Bob was born in the shed in the backyard. Bob and I shared a heritage. He knew it, so every time he saw my truck in the yard, he came and stayed while I worked. He looked at me with understanding eyes, and I talked to him and shared my lunch and snacks. He stayed as long as I did. When I left to go back to Alabama, he left and went back to Bill's house.

One day I made a door for the crawl space hole under the house. I had watched the builders make that kind of door in the bonus room of our new home, so I followed their model. It was two-by-fours nailed onto plywood that fit snugly in the space. The last thing I did was put it in place before driving back to Alabama. When I drove back to the farm the next morning about nine o'clock, my brother said he had just let Bob out from under the house. He heard him howling, trapped under the house. Bob was napping in the cool shade the day before when I put the door in place. I apologized to King Bob and gave him a snack. He forgave me on the spot, and I knew he held no grudge. It was an innocent oversight, and he did get a good night's rest. He stayed with me again that day.

The last time I saw Bob was a sad trip. I went to paint and redecorate the house. I drove up into my brother's yard, and the family was gathering in a circle in the backyard under the maple tree. I joined them, and King Bob was lying on the ground. He was motionless. His eyes were open and set, like he was staring at sights unseen, trying to recognize, organize, comprehend, and understand. We talked quietly. My niece, Betty Anne, placed a handkerchief over his face. My sister-in-law, Jo Anne, fanned him with a magazine cover. My nephew, John, said the vet had done all he could. My brother, Bill, told me the story silently with a glance. Everything said, "The King is Dead".

We took Bob to the yard where he was born, where he ate, played, barked, and reigned. We went to the shed and brought back shovels and picks. We started digging. The hole was wide and deep. Once I said, "We are deep enough." My brother said, "Keep diggin'." The grave was fit for a king, laid out fully for his eternal rest, nothing bent or strained, crowned with respect and dignity. Then, we filled the hole, and piled dirt high to mark the grave. We wept, said goodbye to King Bob, and talked of happy memories. I went and sat in the swing awhile. I knew a chapter had ended that day in our family history.

On my next visit to the farm in Tennessee, I walked to Bob's grave and wondered if I should make a marker, "Here lies King Bob". I recognized the voice. It said, "Bob, come and meet Clark, Herman, Robert, and Sister. I knew no marker was necessary and said as I walked away, "Long Live the King!" Amen.